FIFTY YEARS FLY BY

My Brush with Aviation . . .

WRIGHT BROTHERS MASTER PILOT AWARD 2016

TEMPUS 50 FUGIT

RANDY LIPPINCOTT

RANDY LIPPINCOTT

Order this book online at www.trafford.com
or email orders@trafford.com

Most Trafford titles are also available at major online book retailers.

Print information available on the last page.

ISBN: 978-1-4907-8243-0 (sc)
ISBN: 978-1-4907-8245-4 (hc)
ISBN: 978-1-4907-8244-7 (e)

Library of Congress Control Number: 2017907346

Trafford rev. 05/31/2017

 **PUBLISHING®** www.trafford.com
North America & international
toll-free: 1 888 232 4444 (USA & Canada)
fax: 812 355 4082

Contents

PART FOUR – Arizona

The Last Word

About the Cover

The cover of this book depicts the sky. Indeed, the gossamer covering, like the Earth's atmosphere, will last a lifetime if treated with respect. This gaseous medium has given me life, the joy of freedom, and the privilege of flight. The wild blue yonder has been the road that has guided me through many amazing and thrilling experiences. Like my flight logs, the rugged covering is functional, durable, and designed for frequent use during a reader's lifetime.

The natural pattern on the cover is symbolic of my conservative roots and the hope of fair weather for a safe journey. The acid-free paper should not yellow over time. Stark white, like the glaciers and different snow-covered mountains I have climbed and flown over, these pages hold many of my remarkable aviation experiences. Hopefully, sharing them with you will make them more valuable, and help you understand the path of my perspective.

—Randy Lippincott

As a pilot only two bad things can happen to you (and one of them will):

    a. One day you will walk out to the aircraft, knowing it is your last flight.

    b. One day you will walk out to the aircraft, not knowing it is your last flight.[1]

Science, freedom, beauty, adventure...aviation offers it all.

                       — Charles A. Lindbergh

Aviation is proof that, given the will, we have the capacity to achieve the impossible.

                       — Eddie Rickenbacker

---

[1] http://funnyairlinestories.com/pilot_stuff/pilot_sayings.asp

Dedication

To my parents, Dick and Rosalie Lippincott, for my very early introduction to all things aviation. Also to Johnny Hruban for his patience and skill in teaching me, my family members, and others from my hometown the mastery of flight. His influence has lasted me a lifetime.

And to my gracious wife, Joyce Berk-Lippincott, who has made all that I do in retirement possible. Thank you for standing by me and putting up with the work on my autobiographical trilogy. I could not have accomplished it without your support.

Acknowledgements

This book is the third in my autobiographical trilogy. The first, *Three Days of the Condor,* is about my 36 years of technical rock climbing; the second, *Out of the Blue,* is a faithful autobiography with my professional skydiving career as a sidebar; and this book, *Fifty Years Fly By*, covers my half century of aviation experience. Thanks to my flight instructor Johnny Hruban, I have enjoyed 50 years in the three-dimensional world of flying. Because of his patience and ability to teach a young boy the fundamentals of aviation, I have safely flown 8,000 hours, most of it in the Intermountain West and the remote wilderness of Alaska. This skill has been the basis for exploration, setting the stage in the pursuit of great adventures, and has provided opportunities otherwise unknown to the non-flying public.

My father, Dick Lippincott, had an airplane on the farm and, of course, I learned to fly. It was one of those things that I took for granted. Naturally, as a 16-year-old I knew no fear and had no timetable. The early practice of flight gave me tried, and true lifelong habits and the act of flying became second nature for me. My aviation experience has come in spurts, interrupted by school and the military service. But from the moment of my first aerial excursion at the impressionable age of five, I am still intrigued by the perspective and freedom gained while slipping the surly bonds. Those early flights not only changed my philosophy of life but my entire world.

My mother's story is shorter than my father's but just as intense. However, unlike Dad, my mom was learning on pace with her friend Retha Treptow, and they ended up flying together. Mom's pride of airmanship was fully realized when she flew her mother on a long cross-country trip to Iowa City, Iowa. Rosalie's position usually was in the right front seat and was as supportive of Dad as he was encouraging of her newly earned and exceptional aviation skills at the age of 40. Both of my parents set a positive example for me.

Dale M. Walters was the no-frills station manager with Ryan Air who gave me my big break. Known as the "Arctic Grouch," he helped me survive those critical and stressful times during that first winter north of the Arctic Circle in 1989-90. As the chief pilot in Kotzebue, Dale drew on his 50 years of military and civilian aviation experience in his daily operations. I looked up to Dale and knew that he would test me in more ways than I could imagine. It was an initiation that everyone did not survive.

Foreword by Loren Lippincott

In his latest book, *Fifty Years Fly By*, Randy captures the headiness of flying while embracing the heart and feel of flight. Painting his stories of flight in a way that draws on all of the reader's senses, one feels as though he is right there in the cockpit. Randy shares the extremes of flying from -50° Fahrenheit in Alaska to the desert heat of America's great Southwest; from single engine "first love" adventures to multi-engine challenges; from flight for fun as a private pilot to the rigors of commercial passenger and freight hauling. The combination of Randy's honesty, transparency, and superb detail make for a story that is at the same time fun and enlightening.

The love of flying was instilled in my brother and me as kids when we first learned to fly with our dad, a Nebraska farmer. At age 41, Dick Lippincott decided it was time to fulfill a lifelong dream and learn to fly. Our mother soon followed suit and also earned her pilot's license.

My combined flight time between the United States Air Force and Delta Air Lines is 21,000 hours. Upon graduation from college, I entered the USAF and had 1000+ hours instructing in the T37, 1000+ hours in the F-16, and now 19,000+ hours for Delta Air Lines. I guarantee, as a pilot myself, that whether you are a private, commercial, or military pilot, you will certainly glean "good gouge" from this book that will help make you a better pilot. I know it has for me!

Those of us who are pilots know that on any given day "it could happen to you." Flying produces instant gratification, thrill, and beauty, yet always possesses an ever-present respect, for we are kept aloft by a machine built by humans and flown by fallible humans. Flying is a humbling business, and we are all students in the aviation schoolhouse. Randy passes along his "war stories" that will keep you engaged, and you will take away principles to use in your own "combat" in the air and on the ground.

Over the years of flying with hundreds of pilots in both the USAF and Delta, I have found they all have one thing in common—they LOVE to fly! I've never heard pilots say they would rather do anything else. Flying is truly an ongoing love affair between the pilot and aircraft. However, I think this book goes beyond speaking solely to the pilot and his "lover." I believe Randy captures the mysteries of this love affair for the person who loves the pilot. The significant other for any pilot can read this book and understand the mystical connection between the pilot and his flying machine.

Randy is a "pilot's pilot," and this book is a gift to pilots everywhere. Whether new to aviation, have thousands of hours under your belt, whether you fly for pleasure or profession, or if you are a person who loves a pilot, you will enjoy my brother's book.

Loren Lippincott
Captain Delta Air Lines

Preface

The vast and sublime solitude experienced in aviation is unknown to the earthbound two-dimensional world. For me, flying has been an unchallenged path to freedom for my soul. It was the essential root of the liberation that I appreciated growing up on a farm in Nebraska, which, incidentally, harbored a runway. Over the years, that freedom has become an ingrained part of my nature. The sovereignty of the outdoors, with the wind in one's face, is inherent to man's true spirit. The autonomy that I took for granted was my very salvation from the mundane. My position is possibly a little different from the norm. It is a more focused viewpoint, a real defiance of life's gravity on a grand scale.

My perspective gained through aviation is unmatched in any other discernible realm. Throughout the range of light, it is visually revealing, emotionally exciting, and wonderfully dynamic. These images are unwitnessed by the landlocked masses.

From the moment of my beginning aerial sojourn at the tender age of five, I am still intrigued by the perspective and deliverance gained while looking down on the earth from above. Those early flights not only changed my philosophy of life, but they also helped mold my entire world. At that time, I could not fathom that much later aviation would turn out to be my vocation in the real-life wilds of the Alaskan frontier.

My story starts with my fledgling aerial trials. It seems that my intrinsic need for speed was nurtured early in life. This book follows the story of my aeronautical exposure from paper planes, hanky parachutes, and balsa models, to earning the highest license in aviation—the Airline Transport Pilot (ATP).

My earliest memories include looking down on the green geometric shapes and textures of cultivated fields and prairies in the Midwest, and later the farms dotted with bouquets of brilliant autumn colors.

Early on, I gained access to the bold, truly scenic mountains, rocky spires, and snow-clad summits of the Intermountain West. Later I explored the coastal waters, endless mountain ranges, and vast wilderness areas of Alaska and Western Canada. Much of what I have seen from aloft appeared virgin and untouched by humans.

From above, I have looked down on countless austere, rocky, snow covered peaks, wild, precipitous ramparts, and ridges crowned in giant flowing cornices, commonly surrounded by undulating blankets of milky white clouds. On the job, I was exposed to an endless expanse of rivers and lakes that crossed the horizon; all painted in the shifting hues of cloud shadows. I have surveyed the lifeblood of our nation, the living connection between the snow-capped peaks, forests, and rivers that lead to the far-off oceans. I witnessed the massive buildup of the destructive, yet life-giving cumulonimbus, and played with shadow and light in the boundless airborne reaches of fair weather cumulus clouds. From above, only from the air, can one see how fantastically dynamic the earth's thin crust appears and how it must have changed over time.

Yes, I've seen more than just nature, more than volcanoes, destructive wildfires, and life changing storm fronts. Today I take off and land in metropolitan areas, following the silver wires and blacktops that feed those cities. My aerial vistas have included factories, expansive open-pit mines, and mountaintop observatories. I've flown over the "Boneyard," the Grand Canyon, Mt. McKinley, and the Golden Gate Bridge. I have seen the mark of man for good and bad and witnessed the cycles of nature.

If life is water and time is the stream, then the endless waterway that I have attempted to ford is in the sky. Although unforgiving, the "river's" rewards are beyond the common desire and imagination.

This book contains the stories from my half-century of flight. Some funny, some sad, but most lived on the sharp end of the stick. It has all come full circle for me, from what Wilbur and Orville Wright started at Kill Devil Hills. After all, man is a product of his environment and tools. My adventures in flying have enabled me to experience the tesseract, the fourth dimension within my mind.[2]

My tome includes other stories that I came to know second hand, but nonetheless have influenced me during my lifetime of aviation. I hope that you will find them as moving and exciting as I have. This autobiography is not only about aviation. My life story also brushes on rock climbing and skydiving ventures that involuntarily overlap. These disciplines have their own vocabulary, and to the non-pilot, non-skydiver, or non-climber some of the terms and abbreviations may be confusing. I have endeavored to explain the significance of specialty words when appropriate and tried to use a minimum of technical terms. Your reading experience will be more enjoyable if you embrace them with an open mind. Skim the ones that you do not find curious and "let the story flow." Please feel free to dog-ear the glossary as most of these terms are defined at the end of the book.

---

[2]   https://en.wikipedia.org/wiki/Four-dimensional_space

PART ONE
Nebraska

It called for another spin around the patch

A Boy's Dream

The very thought of that day in 1955 puts me in an ethereal state of happy memories. It was a slow motion movie of the rest of my life. I was five years old when from the front porch of our Nebraska farmhouse, nine miles north of Central City, my brother, my parents, and I watched a Cessna 172 Skyhawk land on State Highway 14 in front of our house. The pilot, whom I had never met, was TV personality Carl Sisskind, my father's shoestring relation by marriage. Accompanying him was my Grandfather Harvey Lippincott.

Carl taxied into our yard that balmy Sunday and changed my global perspective. Before we left, Carl had convinced my parents to let a five-year-old boy and his seven-year-old brother make a seventy-mile maiden flight to Kearney, Nebraska.

Carefully hoisted into the backseat, my brother Jerry and I were buckled in. Carl did his run-up in the driveway and then taxied toward the highway, leaving my dad and pregnant mother behind. When he was sure that the road was clear of traffic, he rolled out onto the two-lane blacktop, and we took off to the north, away from the power lines. We accelerated at a fantastic rate; then when it seemed we could go no faster, we began to float in the air. My heart raced with the increase in altitude; it was all so fantastic and revealing. I thought, "So this is what it is like for the birds." It was impossible to take in everything at first in the three-dimensional adventure. The view from

1

above was so unusual that I wanted more. I recognized most of the neighboring countryside, but now I saw it from an aerial perspective. I had just "slipped the surly bonds of earth," for the very first time! That adventure remains one of my most memorable and life altering to this day.

The big blue sky was cloudless, and the wind was gentle and welcoming. My nose was riveted to the cold Plexiglas window on the left side behind the pilot-in-command. In the calm air, it was truly exciting to see how small the cars on the highway looked, and that the farmhouses and barns all seemed oddly miniaturized from my perch. The topography was laid out in an organized fashion as the roads stretched like guitar strings to the horizon from my bird's eye view. It was the very essence of the Midwest, the rolling and incredible vast expanse of farmland patchwork. From my seat, I believed that I could indeed see the "whole world" as never before. It looked like a giant sized 3-D map of infinite dimensions. For the first time, I could "see over the horizon." I knew at that moment that someday I would take flight as the sole pilot at the controls. I didn't know exactly how then, but the desire for flight was planted in me that day. The fact that my brother was green and puking his guts out in the right-hand seat did not deter from my personal experience.

I remember Grandfather Harvey turning around in his seat, smiling with satisfaction and patting my knee with his large warm hand. We flew over towns and cities, which all looked so neatly laid out and well contained. The villages had common landmarks of water towers, intersecting highways, and railroads. Then all too soon, our cross-country flight came to an abrupt halt when we started our descent to the airport. The airplane had seemed to stand still when at altitude, but closer to the ground I could tell that we were moving very fast. It was my first time to look down on a runway; at first, the blur seemed to approach us cautiously, but then suddenly I heard the sound of the tires chirping as they first touched the concrete. The ride was over, but my brain was still cataloging all the new information. It had been the best field trip a kid had ever experienced. It was the view, the machine, and the pilot whose motions appeared effortless. It was the feeling—the feeling of acceleration, flotation, and then seemingly we were motionless, just sitting in the air. Wow, that was a lot to take in for a five-year-old.

After we had landed in Kearney, my grandfather and Carl drove us to the Greyhound bus depot in the back of a red 1950 Studebaker pickup truck. After lunch, we were left there to wait for the next bus that would take us to Central City. Unsupervised, with only my brother for company, I was still in a state of overwhelming amazement and giddy enthusiasm. I had experienced my first airplane and bus ride at age five. It was my first experience with the compression of travel time through flight. Not bad for a Sunday in Nebraska. That was truly exciting stuff and the genesis of my constant desire for exploration and adventure—a voyage that has lasted a lifetime.

The year before that memorable flight, I became aware of 34-year-old Ann E. Hodges whose left hip was struck by a meteorite while napping on her living room sofa at home. It left a large contusion but did not break the skin. The Sylacauga Meteorite also left an indelible impression on me and piqued my interest in all things space, aviation, and my personal exposure to flight. It was very exciting for me and seemed to strengthen my connection with the unknown and anything off the beaten path. Wow, meteorites didn't just fall to earth in the ancient past, they were real! The meteorite was news of a tangible connection to the unknown and a reminder of the uncertainties that the future holds.

In October 1957, I stood in my pitch-dark country yard looking up at the night sky and had my first glimpse of the Russian satellite Sputnik as it crossed the Milky Way from west to east. It was easy to spot; it was the only "star" racing across the sky, and the viewing times were published in the paper. Slightly to the south, it was an impressive sight. I will never forget the way my realization of a man-made 23-inch sphere in orbit made me feel. How could a gadget launched from Earth look like a star and stay in the sky overhead, night after night? Where was it getting its power? What made it stay up there? Although it only continued to circle the Earth for the next three months, it was overhead every 93 minutes and was traveling at a colossal rate of 18,000 mph. Truly, this was the beginning of the space age, and it was like nothing that man had previously embraced. It was thrilling, and

I wanted to be part of it. As a kid, I started hyperextending my neck, looking up at fluffy clouds, airplanes, contrails, and now nighttime satellites.

The Lippincott Farm - Looking north, State Highway 14 on the left, and the family farmyard foreground, where my first flight at age five took place. Parallel to the highway and on the far right was the location of the Lippincott Private Runway. Photographer Randy Lippincott.

America responded to the launch of the Soviet's first artificial Earth satellite. Werner Von Braun (father of rocket science and the German V1 and V2s that rained down on London during World War II) was now employed by the United States government to help us gain an edge in our ballistic missile design. Von Braun was working for America and tasked by President Kennedy to reach the moon. America fully embraced the space race, and we were in the middle of the cold war. While the development of Intercontinental Ballistic Missiles

(ICBMs) had been the initial objective, our current mission was to put a man into space. And yes, as a child I knew the fear of the atomic bomb, which was reinforced by "duck and cover drills" every time we rehearsed them in school or when I saw a mushroom cloud on TV.

On February 20, 1962, America moved ahead of the Soviets when John H. Glenn Jr. entered Earth orbit. After three trips around the planet, Glenn successfully splashed down in a predetermined area in the Atlantic Ocean. It was the calculated re-entry that would make or break the mission. Enter at a shallow angle and end up lost in space; re-enter at a steep angle, and the untested Mercury capsule would incinerate. There was no established science or math for the computations; the National Aeronautics and Space Administration (NASA) had to figure it out as they went along. Glenn was a fighter pilot in World War II, Korea, Vietnam, a Senator, and the first man to orbit the earth. He was the original badass and later volunteered to go back into space at the age of 77. He passed away at age 95, #Godspeedjohnglenn.

My personal voyage actively started at a very young age on the top tier of my father's windmill, just below the large galvanized weathervane. I was, as many before me, fascinated with flight and all things aerodynamic. I fabricated miniature parachutes for many qualified "feline passengers," climbed the imposing metal structure to the very top, deployed my small unauthorized experiment, and watched it oscillate safely to the ground. It was great fun, and most of them opened nicely.

During my youth, I became fascinated with building and flying balsa model airplanes, both glider and gas powered when I could afford it. I flew large and small aircraft, but the .049 was the standard size gas engine for my budget. The construction was fantastically intense, meticulous work, and helped instill a sense of mechanical aptitude in me. The construction was a type of aviation preschool, and I was the only one in my self-paced class. When not on a mission, these treasures hung from the ceiling in my bedroom as incentives and constant reminders of what was to be. And yes, I watched and was inspired by the old black and white television series called *Sky King*! I wanted to visit the Flying Crown Ranch in Arizona and pilot an aircraft just like the Songbird! The dreamer in me thought that one day I too could pilot a real plane! How thrilling would that be!

In my enthusiasm, I constructed a full-sized rolling cockpit simulator on the east side of the barn. Equipped with various discarded dials, gauges, and control levers, I made up the instrument panel for my "realistic" non-TSO'd cockpit simulator. The single ejection seat was an inverted empty five-gallon tin can that was completely adjustable. No need for power, fuel, flight manual, windscreen, or wings as my imagination took care of all of that for me, and yes, it was stealth—way ahead of its time. I loved the construction work and the stimulation of my imagination in the assembly of all the different components to fabricate a "realistic model." Years later, my younger brother told me that he believed in every detail that the ordinary plywood box was an entirely functional aircraft! Yes, I was a dreamer. Now they claim that aviation dreams are the most common and that flying without the use of an airplane is typically a "positive thing." Those images are supposed to indicate that the dreamer has a high degree of creativity, can rise above the occasion, and demonstrates a certain amount of spiritual maturity. How could I be so lucky!

As a young boy of ten, I vividly recall the *Omaha World Herald*'s article about the discovery of an intact World War II B-24 Liberator in the Sahara Desert. They reported that the thermos in the cockpit still had drinkable coffee in it. The *Lady Be Good* B-24 bomber located in the North African wasteland was a story of remarkable courage and heartbreak in a deadly arena. Out of gas, at night, the entire crew bailed out and perished, thinking they were over the Mediterranean, not the searing and unforgiving sand covered wilderness. They had inadvertently overflown their airfield and continued into the Sahara on a one-way trip. Mysteries like these helped trigger a desire for genuine adventure in me. I was certain that the "wild blue yonder" would be an exhilarating life, like no other, and that untold exciting experiences awaited me. It was the dawning of a new age, and I wanted to be part of it. Somehow, I aspired to explore North America from above and expand my personal limits.

The "Greatest Generation" bred many inspiring aviation heroes. Lindbergh was most likely my personal first because of his grit and record-breaking solo transatlantic flight. I read the story and watched the captivating movie where Jimmy Stewart played Charles A. Lindbergh in the *Spirit of Saint Louis.*

James H. Doolittle was the next most famous and innovative pilot for me. Doolittle was my hero, a pioneer who pushed the envelope, and never gave it a second thought or bragged about it. Jimmy was a test pilot who set records and survived crashes—an example of genuine American exceptionalism. Doolittle inspired his Tokyo Raiders in a daring attack on Japan when he led 16 B-25 Mitchells off a carrier deck. He demonstrated unheard of audacity when he completed an entire flight from takeoff to landing using only his instruments. These were inspirational and motivating stories to a young aviator. It was romantic; it was exciting; it was what I wanted to do. And I knew, later on, that just like Jimmy, *I Could Never Be So Lucky Again.*

The Chuck Yeager story was fantastic; it was *The Right Stuff.* It was all about the exciting rocket-powered Bell X-1 program that we watched unfold on our black and white TV. Yeager was the first to break the sound barrier in *Glamorous Glennis*; not to mention the 12 enemy fighters that he downed to become a double ace during the war.

The Naval Aviator, Dean S. "Diz" Laird, was the only World War II ace who shot down both German and Japanese warplanes and was the only one that I knew personally. Later he became a stunt pilot in the 20th Century Fox film *Tora Tora Tora* in 1969. He flew his 100th aircraft type over Coronado, California, on July 9, 2016, when he was 95. Retired Cmdr. Laird not only served in World War II, Korea, and Vietnam but participated in 175 combat and training missions. He served on 12 different carriers, flew in the Navy's first jet squadron, was the first person to land a jet-powered aircraft aboard the *USS Midway*, but also has the most arrested landings on a straight-deck carrier. He had a great memory and loved to share his stories with anyone who would listen.

During those early years, the favorite draw for my family was any air show where Bob Hoover was performing. Known as the "pilot's pilot," he was a superb aerobatics pilot in his P51 Mustang. However, it was his Shrike Aero Commander that he could make do anything that an airplane could do and make it look easy. Robert A. Hoover had flown in World War II, was shot down over the Mediterranean, and interned as a POW in Stalag Luft 1, Barth, Germany. He escaped from prison, commandeered a Fw-190 (German fighter airplane), and flew himself to freedom after evading the Nazis. Hoover was a great aerobatics pilot but also a brave World War II ace. Now that's guts! Hoover knew Orville Wright, Chuck Yeager, Charles Lindbergh, Eddie Rickenbacker, Jimmy Doolittle, Neil Armstrong, and Yuri Gagarin; he was a living bridge between aviation's Golden Age and today's modern aerospace community. All of these men are authentic American heroes and were inspiring aviators for me.

My father had an airplane on the farm that I learned to fly. I suppose you could say that it was my first "Forest Gump" moment. I knew no fear and yet understood the essential elements of operating real machinery from my work on the farm. The practice gave me tried and true healthy lifelong habits, but the act of flying seemed straightforward, and it was second nature to me from the start. I quickly sensed what the airplane was attempting to tell me, and I was able to control it. At 16, I was a licensed student pilot of my father's Cessna 140 that could easily exceed 120 mph in a shallow dive. My early aviation experience came in spurts; it was interrupted by school, the military service, and the occasional lack of funds, but I always returned to it.

Now, you all know that time goes by more quickly as you age, but do you know why? For example, take me as a four-year-old and the reason I thought summer felt like it took a long time to pass. To me, summer was a very long time; it seemed equal to the rest of the year. At that innocent age, one year was nearly half of my entire "aware" lifetime. Wow! Now that same summer is a mere $1/272^{nd}$ of my existence, hardly any time at all, a flash in the pan! You see, it is just that logical. The numbers don't lie.

Occasionally I've been asked why I fly. I would like to believe that it is my natural skill, but the truth of the matter is that it is genetic. Yes, today we are genetically modified organism (GMO) mills. Our genes have evolved through natural selection over the millennia. During the Pleistocene epoch, Homo Erectus began roaming upright to facilitate hunting in the tall grasses of the savanna; he adapted, to gain security through greater visibility, by walking erect. The successful Stone Age man mastered fire; today that same adaptive and tranquility gene is triggered whenever I stare into a campfire. Gazing into the flames is mesmerizing and comforting now; it meant survival then. Over time, the fittest Homo Sapiens sought the high ground for defense and to strategically position themselves to detect and avoid predators, for they were not always the hunters. Our surviving ancestors prospered and evolved because they had a vista. Today that same view is worth good money in real estate, and the gene lives on. The aviator naturally seeks and expands that same landscape into 360 degrees, compelled by the same unique genetic material. Therefore, the very tendency toward flight for man is genetically predisposed.

Family History of Aviation

My father (Dick) started taking flying lessons in 1964. As a pilot, he was talented and a fast learner, but the written exam turned out to be his nemesis. He was determined, however, and passed the test on his third attempt. I remember those days, and his resolve in the face of defeat, particularly while he was preoccupied working full-time as a farmer and heavy equipment operator, and volunteering on multiple boards. The least possible number of flight hours required for the private license was 40, virtually half solo and half with an instructor. Because the written exam required a minimum wait time before an applicant could repeat the test, Dad was content to continue to fly and log student time without carrying passengers.

On the date of his check-ride, he had an abundant amount of "student flight hours." When Dad presented his logbook to take the practical portion, the examiner said, "You can't have that many hours!" Instructor Johnny Hruban casually took Dad's logbook, tore out the last few pages and handed it back to the examiner with an acceptable number of hours. Dad passed the performance based flight exam with flying colors. My father safely exercised his flight privileges until he turned 65. I asked him why he stopped flying when he retired his license, sold the plane, and never looked back. He explained that he could tell that he was starting to "slow down." In fact, he was exercising the same good judgment that he had used his entire lifetime. I was extremely proud of him for that.

Dad sincerely loved to fly. His passion was to study the land from above and watch the changes that predictably took place every season. But most of all he loved to share his gift with others. In the back of his logbook, he meticulously kept a running list of passengers that he had taken for a ride. Father was proud of his safety record and distinctive personal achievements. Years later, some of those folks who rode along, many for their first flight ever, did so without a door on the plane. The reason was that I wore a parachute and was going to jump as they watched! That ride was a special memory for anyone involved, and occasionally I hear about it, even to this day. The latest was Ron McGuire, and yes, his face lit up as he recalled it all with vivid enthusiasm. He said, "I couldn't believe how fast you fell away from the airplane!"

Father had a traditional windsock on the runway at the farm. I remember the stout box it came in and that I helped him assemble and erect it along the midpoint of the north/south strip. The heavy-duty all-weather orange fabric cone, attached to a sizable galvanized heavy wire frame, was welded to a commercial grade swivel. You could see it from a great distance. I believe that Dad was pleased to have an airstrip marked as a private field on the Nebraska State Sectional, I know I was. The Lippincott Home Field was where we were busy making memories. First with flying, and soon after it was skydiving on the home turf. I have many distinct recollections of those halcyon days in the Cessna 172 and later the Cessna 182 on that most convenient alfalfa runway.

In part, I believe that it was my father's ability to share flight with others that potentiated the love of aviation in our family. Included in my extended family were many aviators; four were military pilots: Harry Pinkerton, Navy Pilot World War II; George Faser, Marine Corps Pilot World War II; Dale Nitzel, Air Force helicopter Pilot, post-Korea; and Loren Lippincott (my brother), Air Force Jet Fighter Pilot, peacetime. Private pilots included Carl Sisskind, my brief mentor; Dick Lippincott, Flying Farmer, and an exceptional jump pilot; Rosalie Lippincott (my mother), pioneer female Flying Farmer; Lawrence Klein, private pilot; Rich Jones, private pilot; Bob Jones, private pilot; and Phil Jones, instrument-rated private pilot. The latter all transitioned through the civilian system, were self-funded, and self-motivated. Dwight Pinkerton soloed and earned his student license but did not go on. Kameron Klein has become an experienced paraglider pilot, and I received my ATP while I lived in Alaska and flew FAR Part 135, professionally in the "bush." Over the years, these fourteen aviators in my family have flown without any serious mishaps or fatalities.

The B-17 Is a Flying Fortress

My mother's aviation story also started at a young age. On August 17, 1943, working outside on the farm with her father, they were irrigating the crops. During a break in the shade, sitting on the ground with a bottle of Royal Crown Cola, halfway between the Grand Island and Kearney Army Airbases, they were watching an occasional B-17, and B-24 fly overhead. Suddenly her attention was drawn to one of three B-17s flying in formation; it was on fire, and then quickly turned wing-up and into a spin. In an instant, the giant plane fell from the sky and burst into a great ball of orange flames and horrible billowing clouds of black smoke. Neighbors, including my mother, rushed to the crash site, but there was nothing to be done except watch the funeral pyre in silent prayer. The tragic event was three days before her 16th birthday.

Over the years, these images never left my mother's thoughts, and she retold us the emotional story when the occasion was right. After considerable research, she identified living family members of the crash victims. Rosalie raised funds for an official State Roadside Marker that was commissioned and reads as follows:

> On August 17, 1943, a B-17F bomber from the Kearney, Nebraska Army Airfield crashed 300 yards south, killing all aboard. The plane was on a

routine training flight before going overseas. Losing their lives were 2nd Lt. Sylvester J. Diebold, Benton, Missouri; 2nd Lt. Ernest H. Endemano, Los Angeles, California; 2nd Lt. John F. Hickey Port Henry, New York; SSgt. Jimmy McEntire, Wharton, Texas; SSgt. Albert Pivkul, West Warren, Massachusetts; Sgt. Cyril B. Butler, Crooksville, Ohio; Sgt. James V. Pollicita, Bridgeport, Connecticut; and Sgt. Frank E. Sampler, College Park, Georgia.

—Nebraska State Historical Society

August 17, 2003, the 60th anniversary of the tragic event, the solemn marker was officially dedicated with many of the crash victim's relatives present. Closure came to those families because of my mother's steadfast commitment and hard work. The ceremony was consecrated with a flyover.

Mom would frequently mention Amelia Earhart and how much she had looked up to her. She was ten years old in 1937 when Amelia Earhart, flying a Lockheed Electra, disappeared on a flight around the world. The newspapers were full of the story for months. She already knew about this famous lady from reading about her in *My Weekly Reader* at school. Earhart set multiple aviation records and wrote best-selling books about her flying career. Amelia had been one of Rosalie's idols, and she wanted to fly just like her; the seed of aviation had been planted in fertile soil. Although Rosalie never became a member of the Ninety-Nines, an organization for female pilots that Amelia helped form, Mom was a member of the International Flying Farmers.

...I Was the Farmer's Wife—Part Time.
I'm up in the sky! I'm flying that plane!
I'm soaring through space! I haven't a name!
—Source Inez Frazell, author unknown

My mother, in fact, was working in quiet desperation. She had chosen to be a farmer's wife but was living a secret life of desire—a yearning to be at the controls of a real airplane. She supported my father's activity and later championed mine. Her eyes lit up when she related her personal story of adventure, but she gazed off into the distance when she described her only real regret. During my skydiving career, I asked her to fly for me to jump. She simply could not bring herself to do it. She was not confident enough in her ability for that complex and emotionally demanding task, especially for a family member. She would not have been able to forgive herself if anything had happened to me while skydiving.

Earn Wings in Flight Training. Left to right, Rosalie Lippincott, Retha Treptow. John Hruban presenting their Private Pilot's Licenses, November 9, 1967. Photo courtesy of the *Central City Republican Nonpareil*.

Solo

As a 16-year-old in 1966, I was learning by example from my parents. I flew from the same turf airfield where both my mother and father had acquired their skills. I practiced and soloed in a tail dragger in nine hours; it was the docile Cessna 140, N2479V. The all silver bird had two large oval green tinted skylights in the ceiling that were unusual and could be distracting for a youngster. While doing the research for this book, I learned that the 1948 Cessna model 140 that I soloed in is still flying in the Dallas, Texas, area to this very day. Wow, it's been in the air longer than I have!

I was anxious to solo and trusted my instructor Johnny Hruban enough to know that he was going to teach me all that I needed to be successful. I had learned climbs, banks, and descents, along with power management and stalls. He tried to teach me that the control wheel adjusted for airspeed and the throttle was used to climb and descend. I understood the safety and function of the traffic pattern and how to use it as a cue for power and flap settings in preparation to land. During repeated takeoffs and landings, I became familiar with how the runway should look during my approach to landing. The final critical piece of the puzzle was the landing flare. If you didn't get that right, then everything else was useless. Rotate too late, and you bounced off the runway and violently back into the air. Pitch up too early, and you stall above the ground, crash into it and bend the landing gear, or worse yet, flip over out of control.

I had excellent motor skills for an adolescent, along with a daring attitude—no fear. The mechanical apparatus was my friend, and I was in control. With a little exposure and practice, I easily mastered the routine operation of the air machine. Now with a bit of rehearsal, I could land with predictable success. My instructor knew that the time was right, and I had "mastered" the basics. Regardless, it was a bit of a surprise when Johnny told me to come to a full stop and let him out in the middle of the runway. At first, I wondered why he would want to get out of the plane, and then I realized that he wanted me to solo. It's like a threshold that you've been working toward, but never imagined how it was going to look when you got there. It was only momentarily awkward for me.

Okay, I was a bit surprised, but I had been doing it all along. It was just that Johnny had always been with me acting as my safety net. Now I was supposed to do it all: preflight the airplane, run the checklist, make my announcements on the radio, AND look and listen for other traffic, taxi and take off—no problem. Oh yeah! And then land without bending the airplane. Soloing is when the student pilot does three circuits in the traffic pattern accompanied by three takeoff and landings to a full stop as the sole occupant of the plane. I remembered that my mother excitedly told her lady friends that she soloed in the airplane, and they asked, "Rosalie, where did you go?" This question exposes the genuine gap in perception and knowledge between the aviator and the naïve masses. Soloing is the first time you truly perform a series of takeoff and landings all by yourself; you don't leave the pattern at the airport, and you don't GO anywhere. It is an operational benchmark in your student training and the real beginning of the learning process.

Ready for my first solo flight at the south end of the runway, I did my run-up, and a 360 degree turn to carefully look for other airplanes that might be in the traffic pattern and not have a radio. When I saw that it was clear, I lined up at the end and released the brakes as I smoothly applied the power. Thinking back on it today, I was a 16-year-old kid ready to fly an airplane for the first time by myself. I had no video game training for this; it was all real-world activity with actual consequences. As I started rolling down the forgiving grass runway, I noted that my airspeed was "alive." Next, I applied slight forward pressure on the yoke and raised the tail off the ground with little effort. With only modest back pressure on the control wheel, at the prescribed airspeed, I sprang off the tiny airstrip. Wow, the airplane was extremely responsive without Johnny as my passenger. I could tell that it made a striking difference in the aircraft performance as I adjusted the trim tab for the climb-out.

In a minute, I was at pattern altitude turning onto my crosswind leg. I brought the power back and continued the downwind leg, now well established in the traffic pattern. I had just enough time to readjust my trim, glance at the windsock and note that it was still flaccid. Directly abeam my touch-down point, I adjusted the power, applied full carburetor heat, and my first notch of flaps. The small Cessna started to slow and then descend; I was at the prescribed 500-foot level when I turned onto the base leg. Okay, so far so good. I was doing it just like I had learned with Johnny at my side. It was already a natural routine for me. Unfortunately, I started my turn onto final late and had to correct back as I applied full flaps and adjusted my airspeed. My altitude looked good; the runway picture was nearly perfect—even if the power quit right then, I could still land on the field. As I approached the end of the runway, I pulled the power back and gracefully settled onto the "centerline" of the grass runway. Whew, that was actually kind of fun! Now I had to do it two more times to make it count as a full solo. And just like that, with small variations, it came to pass. My mother described it best in her story "Who Me, Fly An Airplane?" when she said, "I am unable to describe the solo flight—that singular, solitary performance intended for one, an experience you cannot share."

Johnny was there to congratulate me and endorsed the back of my student license along with my logbook. I was officially cleared to fly solo in my father's Cessna 140. However, just like taking the gun to go hunting, I needed to ask permission to use it, put it back the way I found it, and promise not to shoot a neighbor—but in this case, promise not to crash into anyone's barn. Well, maybe it wasn't exactly like that, but I could practice takeoff and landings by myself all day long. That meant unsupervised; so I had to fuel the plane by myself before I put it back in the hangar and record the exact amount in the fuel log—and do it all without bending or scratching the airplane. During this time, I learned to prioritize the three components of aviation: aviate, my priority was to fly the plane; navigate, know where I was and where I wanted to go; and communicate, talk on the radio when it was appropriate, but listen all the time.

Student Pilot Certificate, issued June 12, 1966.
Photographer Randy Lippincott.

Soon Dad upgraded to a Cessna 172 (N8239U), and I also soloed in that on the Central City Field. I distinctly remember that day; it was the same familiar north runway, and I was in a T-shirt, blue jean cutoffs, and flip-flops. The routine for runway 33 was a standard left-hand traffic pattern. The counterclockwise traffic is the norm because the pilot in command sits in the left seat and can see where he's going when he turns to the left. It's a safety thing. But in addition to that, the plane naturally wants to turn left. The left turning tendencies come from: 1) the torque effect from engine; 2) P-factor, also called asymmetric propeller loading; 3) gyroscopic precession, when energy is applied to the propeller, its force is generated 90 degrees in the direction of the propeller's rotation; 4) spiraling slipstream, because the propeller is moving fast, and the airplane is moving relatively slow, causing the air to curve around the fuselage and strike the left side of the tail. This force makes the aircraft yaw or tends to turn left.

These flights were the beginning of a very long love affair, and I owe it all to my parents. While my solo flights could not be a destination, but rather they were "in the pattern" or local, nearby to

17

practice student maneuvers including stalls and turns around a point. As a young man, I did not always follow the rules exactly. On some of those flights, I would fly out over the farm. On the way, there could have been some benign looking small clouds, and maybe I had to get a real close look and possibly even see inside one—you know, just a little. It is like the exciting initial time you get to first base as a teenager; right away, you are inclined to "steal" second.

My father started me on heavy machinery at age ten. On the farm, I had operated the D-4 Caterpillar, the John Deere and Ford tractors, the three wheel Cushman, a motorcycle, an automobile, the 1949 F-100 flatbed truck, and then came the airplane. Flight hours the first few years were sporadic, but my enthusiasm never waned. Work on the farm always came first. Next, it was academics, and then sports. Time and money for aviation were low on the priority list, and my progress was slow at first. Two steps forward and one step back for a struggling farm-boy. During those early growing years, I earned 35¢ per hour.

At home, even while I was working in the field on the tractor, I was reminded of aviation. When I looked up in the sky, I could occasionally see a jet, but more likely only the contrail. Even a careful observer would hardly notice chaff on the ground where I was working the soil. To the untrained eye, it looked like a single aberrant strand of traditional tinsel. In fact, it was a radar countermeasure in which military aircraft or other targets spread a cloud of small, thin pieces of aluminum, metalized glass fiber or plastic, which either appeared as a cluster of primary targets on radar screens or swamped the screen with multiple returns. It was an occasional reminder of my long term goal. I wanted to be up in the sky looking down on the vast expanse of the Midwest, winging somewhere beyond the horizon.

Until I started to review my logbooks, I did not realize that my first solo cross-country flight was the same route and in the same type of airplane as my initial flight as a passenger at the age of five. It was in a Cessna 172 from Central City to Kearney, Nebraska, just like I had done 11 years earlier with Carl Sisskind as the pilot. However, this time I departed from the airport and not the highway in front of my house. I had flown nearly 30 hours in Nebraska before my training was interrupted by the military service in Europe.

Dick Lippincott—Our Family Stories

The Lippincotts flew long enough to form some amazing traditions. One was skydiving, and another was buzzing the homestead or an acquaintance. We did not execute a low-level pass with cars on the highway or our neighbors' homes, but we made some low-level, high speed passes on our farmyard. Even when you are outside, typically you will not hear a fast approaching aircraft until it is already upon you. Of course, that first pass was from an altitude, and most of the excess speed bled off when Dad pulled up but was still low enough to survey the countryside up close. By the time he was a mile north, over Prairie Creek and made a course reversal back to the south, Mom was already waiting out in the yard. Now, to make sure that Dad noticed her presence, the most timely article to signal him with was her blouse. And when Dad came back over the barn, there she was in all her glory waving the garment wildly over her head. Before Dick got back to town, the word was out that Mother was frantically waving her bra at Dad; well, maybe it was hard to see such detail at those high speeds.

Dad and his partner in the plane, Doctor Ken Treptow, planned to take Ken's son Warren and me to a Science Fair in Dallas, Texas. We were scheduled to land at Love Field in Dallas. Love was a big, busy airport, and we were vectored to land between two intimidating (and fast) commercial jet airplanes. Since Dick was the flying pilot and Ken was on the radio, there were a few tense seconds after touchdown. Dick and Ken had both read about wake turbulence generated by the big jets but had no real experience with it. All Dad wanted to do was get the hell out of the way of the huge commercial airliner bearing down on us. While Dad felt that the tower was not going to let us be run over by the massive jet plane, he was going to do everything possible to make that first turnoff on the large runway. Even though we had a few anxious moments, it all worked out. Dad had things under control. He handled the aircraft like a pro, and the outcome was never in doubt.

Dick did have a harrowing trip when he brought Jean Steckmyer and Bill Pullen back from Dodge City, Kansas, in exceedingly windy conditions. He said, "I had my hands full flying the plane on that trip." Mom prayed all day for their safe return. Then unexpectedly before Dad arrived in Central City, Mom became aware of a nearby "weather-related" air fatality. On the radio, she heard that a friend, Ralph Beermann, had been killed in his Beechcraft Bonanza attempting to land at Norfolk. It was not until much later that we learned that Ralph crashed due to a heart attack, and the wind had nothing to do with it, but at the time it certainly fueled Mother's anxiety.

Father was a great one for telling stories on himself. He often went out after a full day of farm labor and did touch and goes to relax and maintain proficiency. On one particular outing, Dick was making takeoff and landings when he heard an unexpected noise upon touchdown but couldn't figure out what it was and promptly dismissed it. At the end of his practice session, Dad was ready to park the airplane in the hanger but was unable to locate the tow-bar to help steer it into position. Then he suddenly realized what the noise must have been. Dad walked directly to the waiting red tow-bar on the edge of the runway where he had heard the abrupt sound. Somehow Dad flew well enough that the bar did not strike the propeller or for that matter damage anything else. He never made that mistake again.

The story goes that a young passenger in the back seat asked my parents in the front seats if they had ever had any close calls? Mom turned and answered, "Why yes, we just had one!" Mom and Dad were flying south of Aurora, Nebraska, at about 2,500 feet when a B-52 Stratofortress on a low-level training mission flew directly in front of them on an intercept course. Dad's quick action evasive maneuver was a "duck under" technique. They could look right up at the bomb bay doors. If they had been below and behind the huge jet, the violent wake turbulence would have flipped them over and out of control in an instant. It could not have been any closer to a life-changing disaster. The surprising thing was Dad's quick reaction and that it was over before anyone could be concerned.

B-52s sometimes referred to as "Buff," dominated our lives throughout the cold war. One of the principal missions during the 1960s was called Operation Chrome Dome. As a deterrence, one or more Stratofortesses armed with thermonuclear weapons was continuously on station, flying routes to points along the Soviet Union border. These B-52s were poised to strike or counterstrike at a moment's notice. Later, Vietnam also required the presence of the iconic B-52 with the strategy of carpet bombing. The B-52 was a big part of the Gulf War, and even now while the Air Force is planning a new bomber, It has scheduled to keep the B-52H in service until 2045, nearly 90 years after the B-52 first entered service, an unprecedented length of service for any aircraft, civilian or military.

I remember the look of pleasure on Dad's face when he was taking a passenger for their first airplane ride in the Cessna 182—what joy he got from that! He also loved having tickets on "Lil' Birdie Airline" for folks to bid on at the Fairview Church Harvest Auction fundraiser. He always encouraged Mom and was happy to let her fly the family bird when they traveled anywhere.

Rosalie related the account of our neighbors, Neal and Agnes Hartford's inaugural flight. Agnes was scared stiff because it was her first-ever airplane trip and she was in her eighth decade. Reluctantly, Agnes got in the backseat with Mom for the daredevil ride. Right away she tucked her head down inside her jacket and closed her eyes. All you could see was a mop of gray-streaked hair where her face should have been. She believed that it was going to be her last day on earth. After they had been airborne awhile, Dick headed toward the Hartford farm. Rosalie leaned over and told Agnes, "If you would peek out the window, you'll see your farmhouse." Tentatively, Agnes glanced out the window over her jacket and then took a good heads-up look. The rest of the flight she was carefully watching everything there was to see. They landed and were getting ready to deplane when Agnes turned to Rosalie and said, "To think, I missed the first part of the flight." Mom gave her a big hug as if to say, "Welcome to the family."

Rosalie and Dick Lippincott in front of the Cessna 182, circa 1971.
Photographer unknown.

One day Father took the neighborhood preacher and his wife on a local sightseeing flight. When they returned to the airport, the couples' young mentally challenged daughter anxiously asked her parents, "Did you see God?" Flying even evoked great things in the innocent.

A high school classmate, Larry Gee, had flown home from college for "Homecoming" and offered to take me up in his tiny rented Cessna 150. It was Saturday, November 4, 1972, and I "jumped at the chance," of course, pun intended! I had just returned home from the Army, and my initial civilian skydive would be at the Central City Airport in his small Cessna. Overall, it was pretty uneventful with a 20-second delay from 5,400 feet, and I was alone. Of course, the real trick was getting my bulky parachute rig past the control column and safely out the door of the tight cockpit that had a narrow bench seat. I was happy to see and interact with Larry under those momentous conditions. It was an odd connection, to say the least, with Gee as the pilot and me the skydiver/pilot. Larry was always friendly, wore a smile, and was an excellent student. Having grown up on a farm, he wasn't afraid of hard work. Larry was big, a lot taller than me, and we had played high school sports together.

Three days later, on Tuesday, November 7, 1972, he was to fly back to the South Dakota School of Mines in Rapid City where he was finishing his degree. That evening, as dark clouds continued to gather, we discovered tragedy had struck. It had been a widely overcast Midwestern day when Larry departed Central City. In Nebraska, the terrain rises as you head northwest. Gee wasn't licensed to fly into the clouds (instrument flight rules or IFR), so he stayed under them. Eventually, it caught up with him in the Sandhills. He was flying under and around low-lying clouds (scud running) and flew into the side of a grassy basin during cruise flight. He died instantly. The accident is called controlled flight into rising terrain (CFIT) by the National Transportation and Safety Board (NTSB) and is a common low-time pilot mistake. The real irony was that the parachute I had used on the previous flight could have saved his life.

My father and his partner in our airplane, Dr. Ken Treptow, were part of the search team that found Larry's body. It was a very gloomy day following my welcome home skydive. I didn't have my logbook with me at the time, so I did not get Larry's signature for that jump. It would have been comforting to be able to look at it now and then. The Lutheran Church in Central City was overflowing for his funeral. It makes me melancholy to this very day to think about it. Larry was a good man, had a gentle soul, and I still miss him all these years later.

Dad didn't like to fly very high, and it took several years to get him to 10,000 feet for me to skydive from his plane—and then only on special occasions. He loved to fly low-level to check out the fields and to be closer to Mother Earth. For whatever reason, he felt more comfortable closer to the ground. Many of our neighbors could testify to that. Father had spent his entire life working the land and loved to monitor the soil and crops from above, but still up close at hand. Often, while doing so, he would spy an unsuspecting neighbor (Marland Beckstrom) in the field on his tractor diligently toiling in his crops. Dad would maneuver around behind the target, about ten feet off the deck at 120 mph. The result was predictable and always given and received in good temperament! The only thing that was truly affected was the recipient's laundry. Marland was also a pilot and to reciprocate was the only rational response. My father was a lifelong safe pilot but liked to have fun, and family skydiving seemed to fall squarely into the second category.

On occasion when the time of day was right, Dad would use the plane to check on the status of irrigation water in the tall fields of corn. It was a most expeditious and thorough way to note dry or flooded areas in otherwise obscure portions of maturing crops. On the other hand, it was a way to help the neighbor who needed his assistance with locating missing cows or a frisky bull. Dad could easily spot rambunctious cattle even in the tallest of cornfields, and make short work of the roundup.

911 Was Busy

I was on leave from the Army in 1971, and it was the end of the week; Father had set aside time to fly for me to skydive at the farm. The convenience of having our plane, runway, and built in drop zone was huge. However, the time had gotten away from us when I noticed that it was 6:30 and I had a 7:00 p.m. date with Ginger who lived 17 miles away. The last eight of those miles were on a gravel road. I conferred with Dad, and he agreed that the quickest way to get there was by air; however, they did not have a runway on their property.

With the planned shortcut I estimated that I would only be 15 minutes late. I called Ginger Uzendoski with the new schedule, but gave no real explanation, "Stand out in the middle of the yard at 7:15 and I will be there." Hurriedly, I showered, dressed, and drove back out to the runway and the waiting Cessna. I threw on my parachute, and we were in the air in no time. It was to be my 6th jump of the day! Dad knew right where to fly, and we were quickly at 5,300 feet over Ginger's farm at the prescribed time. Since I had been jumping all afternoon, I knew how to gauge the winds. I gave Dad a couple of directional corrections, and then he cut the engine to decrease our airspeed. Slowing down made it easier for me to open the door for a clean exit. In a flash, I was in freefall for a 20-second delay and uneventfully deployed the old surplus 28-foot modified orange and white canopy. After my departure, Dad did a wingover and headed for home low-level, where he was most comfortable flying. I landed in the horse corral, a little short of the big tree-lined farmyard with all of those messy power lines, where my date was waiting for me.

Ginger was thrilled and impressed by the uniqueness of my little escapade. In just a few minutes I field packed my parachute, zipped off my jumpsuit James Bond style, and threw them in the trunk of her car. Not thinking anything of my jump, we headed into Fullerton and then on to dinner and a movie in Grand Island. Halfway into town, we met the entire volunteer fire department and rescue trucks; hell bent on the way to a catastrophic accident! As the dust cleared, we pulled back onto the gravel road, turned to each other and said that we hadn't seen any indication of a fire anywhere. We wondered where all the trucks were heading. Wow, whatever it was, it must be big to demand that amount of fanfare!

As it turned out, the next day Ginger called me with an update, saying that a neighbor had called in the emergency. They saw an airplane go down, "Cause they heard the engine abruptly 'stall,' saw the pilot bail out, plummet through the air and deploy his emergency parachute!" Then the plane suddenly turned and dove toward the ground. They didn't know exactly where the impact site was. I guess the fire chief thought they would just drive around long enough until they spotted a guy hitchhiking with a parachute over his shoulder or saw a column of black smoke from the wreckage. After all, everyone knows that airplanes always burst into flames and black smoke when they crash. It shouldn't be that hard to spot in broad daylight! What they needed was another airplane to find the "crash site." They were looking for me, and I was feeling a bit sheepish!

Needless to say, I never pulled that little impromptu stunt again in Nance County. I didn't want to have to deal with the Polish authorities or get my name in the paper. I knew that with enough time they would figure it out and be red-faced. I didn't want to be there to have to answer any questions.

Both of my parents belonged to the International Flying Farmers. They made many trips together and enjoyed hosting the farm organization at their home field. It was the summation of everything that Dad had worked toward his entire life, and it was fulfilling for both of them. Mom came up with the local flying club name when she used the runway heading for the 15-33 Club. Today, enough time has passed for the magnetic heading of the runway to fluctuate causing the numbers to change. Currently, the runway heading at the Central City airport is 16-34. Yes, this could give one pause to think that the magnetic north pole has shifted that much during my lifetime. And, yes, the runway is now concrete instead of grass. No more worrying about getting mired down in mud during the monsoon season.

One year Dad made the trip to Oshkosh for the annual national fly-in. For this once in a lifetime event, there were two other pilots in the 182 and one non-pilot. Everything was going great, but they had to make a planned stop for gas. Ten miles out, they called the tower and received landing instructions for "straight in" runway 09. As they approached the field, Dad knew that he was landing to the east, and touched down uneventfully. As they taxied clear of the runway, Dad noticed that he had mistakenly landed on a taxiway and, in fact, there wasn't even a tower on the field. It took three pilots to land at the wrong airport without even using a runway. No harm, no foul, and the fuel was cheaper than expected.

A brief explanation of runways indicates that they are labeled with a number from 01 to 36, which designate magnetic headings in ten-degree increments. When taking off or landing to the east the runway would be marked with 09, or ninety degrees in big white numbers at the nearest end. Landing on the same runway but in the opposite direction would be identified 27, or 270 degrees. When landing to the south, the marking would indicate 18, or 180 degrees, etc. If there are parallel runways, they are designated R and L, like 09R and 09L.

Another story about almost landing on the wrong airfield involves my brother Loren. He was a T-37 instructor pilot at Vance Air Force Base in Enid, Oklahoma, and while he was sitting next to his student, they started to land at the wrong airfield while on a cross-country trip. Almost instantly, but too late, Loren recognized that they were at the wrong airport and abruptly gave the student "Go-Around" instructions. Instead of ultimately landing, it turned into a high-speed flyby. So off they went to an "alternate airport." The student never had any idea about what had just happened, and Loren never told him.

Luckily, I can say that I have never landed or even been close to landing at the wrong airfield, even in Alaska's vast "outback." I always took pride in my piloting. Where I flew commercially in Alaska, it was a challenge because most of my flights were by dead-reckoning only; in the cold and dark, snow covered unfamiliar country, during poor weather. I may not be doing that any longer, but wouldn't have traded the experience for anything.

I Learned about Flying from That

We were skydiving on North 48ᵗʰ Street at Arrow Field in Lincoln, Nebraska in 1973. It was the first flight of the day and a cold start for the Cessna 185. I was the last one in and, therefore, the person sitting next to the updated in-flight door. Unlike the standard door, it hinged upward under the wing when opened. Marv Helman primed and cranked the big Cessna engine several times, then primed again until it backfired. The 185 caught fire, and flames licked the side of the airplane past my window and instantly shot fear into everyone.

I recalled the same thing had occurred during a winter cold-start when I was with my dad years before in Central City. The frosty start for aircraft engines is a problem from three aspects: First, the air-cooled engine is constructed from dissimilar metals that contract and expand at different rates when cold; therefore, the pistons bind and cause excessive friction on startup (preheat should be applied as indicated by the manufacturer). Second, the oil is viscous and does not lubricate well at low temperatures, causing additional friction. Third, when the battery is cold, it simply does not have the cranking power for a typical start.

It was winter time. Dad and I had the plane out of the hanger pointed south and after multiple attempts to start it, the carburetor flooded and spilled gas onto the surrounding cowling. The engine subsequently backfired and ignited the raw gasoline that sat inside the engine compartment just waiting to burst into flames. Without speaking, I sprang into action as soon as I saw the flames coming out of the engine compartment. I vaulted out of my door and started scooping up snow with my bare hands. I was shoving it into the large oil access door on the right-hand side of the old Cessna as fast as I could. In just a minute the flames turned into white plumes of steam. I had saved the aircraft and avoided a tragic situation. Dad had run to the end of the hangar to phone the fire department. That day in Lincoln, with the Cessna 185, the same old reflexes were triggered.

As soon as I saw what was happening to the Club's 185, I jumped out of the right-hand door and in two steps began addressing the source of the flames. It had only ignited excess fuel inside the large exhaust pipe that projected well out of the right side of the cowling and was truly self-limited. The typical protocol for this scenario is to continue cranking the motor, and the flames are sucked back into the engine—no problem. However I was fixated on the issue, and while standing in the arc of the propeller, I thrust my well-protected right forearm against the flaming orifice. I extinguished the flames instantly. To ensure that the fire did not reappear I held my arm in place a moment longer. All the while I was so focused on the matter that I did not recognize my vulnerable position directly in line with the deadly blades.

I surveyed the situation for only an additional fleeting second. Then, when I felt assured of the safety of the jumpers and the aircraft, I started to step back to signal Marv that I had it under control. At that EXACT instant, barely outside of the killing zone, I felt the rush of the large and lethal 86-inch long cleaver pass close enough to my face to know that I was, in fact, still alive. Then, with a surge, the engine roared to life. The exhaust spewed black smoke as a sacrifice for my life. The gasoline/air mixture, at last, had been ignited in just the correct proportion for continuous combustion. My desire to jump suddenly took flight that day.

I felt that my "guardian angel" had moved me aside at the very last millisecond, or, at least, had her hand on the aircraft ignition. Nothing less than a force field protected me from the deadly blade. Never had anything that life-threatening come that close to instantly killing me except maybe when I was hit by a car on my motorcycle. My heart was already racing as I started to breathe again and I was so very thankful that my head was still located on my shoulders. My helmet would have only become a vessel to contain the gray-matter. Unable to see me from his seat on the plane, Marv had no idea what had just happened. We made the jump, but I had no enthusiasm to continue that day. I needed a respite to contemplate the future and count my blessings.

After the military service, I resumed my flying lessons in Lincoln, Nebraska. I flew that summer until I had surgery on my back. My recovery was lengthy, and it wasn't until the next summer that I resumed my lessons in Salt Lake City, Utah, where I earned my private pilot's license.

While my brother Loren was in the Air National Guard following his active duty service in the Air Force. He was proud of his 1,000 hours as pilot in command (PIC) of the Fighting Falcon F-16. At an opportune time one day he phoned Mom and Dad and advised them to call some neighbors to join them for an air show over the old runway at the farm. He had intended to make a small unsanctioned detour from his assigned mission, and it was going to be on Uncle Sam's nickel. At the prescribed time, Loren and his rogue F-16 buddy made a high-speed, low-level pass over the farm coming from opposite directions. They went inverted, they went vertical, and they made incredibly tight 360 degree low-level turns in full afterburner around stage center. At the climax of the show, Loren was "on the deck" heading directly toward the crowd but pulled maximum Gs at the last second and turned straight up and spiraled out of sight. This last impressive show of brute force sprayed the small gathering with dirt and jet-blast; it was that close to the unsuspecting audience. One of the children in attendance later had nightmares following the ear-splitting, earth shaking display of power. It was the best air show that Merrick County or Mead Township had ever witnessed. Later, Mom learned that neighbors who were not in attendance called the sheriff's office with reports of being attacked by some hostile Air Force, and it had spooked their cattle too. The sheriff knew who was doing the flying and had no intentions to follow-up on the complaint.

PART TWO
Utah

Wasatch Checkride, The First of Many

I passed my written test in 1974 without any difficulty, had flown the required hours, and was signed off for my Federal Aviation Administration (FAA) Private Pilot checkride. The solo cross-country trip had been from Salt Lake City Airport #2 to Delta in the West Desert, then through the Pahvant Range, Kanosh Pass, to Richfield in a narrow valley, and back to #2. It was a large triangle, and each landing had to be accompanied by a local endorsement to document that I had physically landed there. With all of the prerequisite material in hand, I met with the FAA examiner for the oral portion of the test. I felt confident and proceeded to the practical part of the examination. I carefully laid out the assigned flight plan that included a full FAA Flight Service Station standard briefing including weather and winds aloft. There was no time limit on this portion of the exam, and I left no stone unturned. My calculations included visual enroute checkpoints and exact times for each on the entire proposed trip. I had been taught to pay attention to detail from the very beginning of my flight training and used the E6B computer to determine my magnetic heading and ground speed for the trip.

Once I completed those tasks successfully, the examiner accompanied me to the aircraft where I performed and explained my detailed preflight check. After that exercise, I escorted the examiner to his seat on the plane, made sure that he had his seatbelt securely fastened and gave him a full passenger briefing. I dutifully used the checklist and after start-up made all the appropriate radio calls.

Next, I taxied out, took off, and climbed to the predetermined altitude for the flight-plan route. When established on-course, and it looked like I knew what I was doing, he gave me new instructions. The examiner had me repeat all the necessary maneuvers that I had learned in training. When we returned to the field, he had me demonstrate the various types of landings and takeoffs with and without flaps. Once I made the last landing, I was relatively confident, and I received my temporary Private Airman's Certificate. Now I was able to carry passengers. I was no longer a student pilot, but of course, in reality, this was merely a license to begin a lifetime of education. I learned about aviation weather, troubleshooting, and most of all, trained in sound decision making. I didn't know it then, but it was the first of many checkrides that I would submit to over a lifetime. I had no idea that those formal sessions were going to continue for the next half century.

Left to right, FAA examiner, Randy Lippincott, my flight instructor at Airport #2, Salt Lake City, Utah, June 20, 1974—the day of my Private Pilot checkride in a Cessna 150. Photographer unknown.

All of the previous hours were to teach me the fundamentals of the stick and rudder. They were the components of climbing, descending, straight and level flight, and coordinated turns. The rudder does not turn the airplane the way a boat rudder works on the water. When used with the turn and bank indicator, the rudder supplements or coordinates the turn along with the wings. I learned, early on, how to feel what the airplane was trying to tell me. I was discovering the hidden secret of all heavier-than-air flight, which was the angle of attack and how it relates to airspeed. That airspeed is the key element; without it, the airplane was only going down. I not only could identify a stall, but feel how close I was to one. The stall is when the wing loses lift, NOT when the engine sputters. Through repetition, my practice taught me what the runway should look like on approach. Johnny taught me early on that the throttle managed altitude and the elevator controlled airspeed. In emergencies, you must already know your best glide airspeed. During the descent, by pointing the nose in a shallow configuration, the aircraft descends more steeply. By pointing the nose down more steeply, the glide is paradoxically increased. In aircraft with variable pitch propellers, changing to the most course pitch or low RPM (feathering the prop) will also extend the glide considerably, as the wind resistance is decreased.

My early flights were primarily in the vicinity of and over Salt Lake City since I was taking off from an airfield within the city. Without any formal instruction, I increased my activity to night flights over the vast populated area that spread along the extensive and beautiful Wasatch Range. The sea of city lights was alluring at night and made for a smooth and safe transition. I quickly became comfortable flying along the mountainous Wasatch Front during the day and found it even more enjoyable at night over the expanse of friendly metropolitan illumination. The caveat was that much of my hazardous aeronautical work was in the proximity of mountainous terrain. With increased exposure, I gradually learned the nature of mountains and their intimate relationship with the wind and weather. I had many nighttime clues to learn and master since the margin of safety at night is considerably more narrow. Also, there are illusions at night to consider and understand. Many judgment calls in the dark were regarding weather, visibility, and crossing rising terrain. I soon learned about black holes and how to judge whether my altitude was adequate to clear them. Nighttime planning was critical, and instrument techniques were necessary when there was NO outside reference to a horizon. The lack of a visual reference was the tragic and often repeated mistake by many pilots of spatial disorientation and subsequent loss of aircraft control when there was no outside background for comparison.

It wasn't long until I ventured over the massive open pit Kennecott copper mine (Bingham Canyon Mine) just outside Salt Lake City, Utah. Now called the Rio-Tinto-Kennecott mine, it is a blight on the Oquirrh Mountains—a massive manmade divot that changed the landscape. But what a fantastic birds-eye view of a gigantic, austere, circular pit! Intimidating enough that I did not fly very far down inside the mine. If something happened, there would be no escape. I did not want to repeat the mistake that the two airline pilots in the rented Cessna 150 made when they crashed into the bottom of the Meteor Crater in Northern Arizona. I'm sure there were some regulations about it somewhere. It most likely fell under the "Stupid Rule," which says not to anything stupid when you are flying an airplane. You will pay for it.

Rio-Tinto-Kennecott Mine, the Oquirrh Mountains, southwest of Salt Lake City, Utah. Photographer Randy Lippincott.

Those flights took me to many wonderful and scenic places throughout the West. While in Utah, when I had the available funds, I was skydiving at Cedar Valley, south of Salt Lake City. In due time, I volunteered to fly the 182 for jumpers. Young and foolish, I quickly became bored with the familiar up-and-down pattern and orbiting at altitude. Since I did not want to "cold-shock" the engine while diving the plane, I chose to practice my rolls and spins on the way down. A barrel roll should only generate a minimum G-force. If not done perfectly a negative G could be triggered. In this case, the dirt would come off the floor and into my face. What I did not realize was that battery acid also could spill out of the aviation filler caps. That minor offense cost me my volunteer job and many hours of free flight time. I only had a total of ten hours logged flying jumpers at Cedar Valley off the remote little dirt runway.

Around that same time, however, another jump pilot struck a parked car with an airplane. My personal feelings were tempered when I heard about the not-so-super "Buzz Story" which was all hearsay, of course, because I did not physically witness it. Apparently, after dropping a load of jumpers out of a Twin Beech, the pilot, who went by the name of Buzz, flew over the DZ parking lot at a high rate of speed and right on the deck. A "buzz job" is a celebratory tradition, and gained notoriety in the movie *Top Gun*. It is not necessarily considered marginal behavior, but it is usually carried out over the central runway complex, and people should not be at risk. That day the airplane's propeller made significant contact with the top of a parked car. It was notable enough to make it look like a sliced tomato. At the very minimum, any aircraft would require a complete engine teardown, inspection of the crankshaft, and a new expensive propeller—a very pricey proposition for a mere few seconds of celebration!

I'm sure that it cost more to rebuild the engine and replace the car than removing a little acid corrosion from a battery spill. Allegedly, the damaged car was purchased on the spot and quietly buried at an undisclosed location nearby in the remote desert under cover of darkness. It almost sounded like a Mafia-style execution and secret wilderness burial with the help of an illicit backhoe. I'm sure the car is still well hidden and all that's left today is a small rusty depression in the barren sand and an automobile title that was never transferred. However, when discovered by a future archaeologist, I'm certain the VIN numbers will still be identifiable.

Therefore, if the incident was reported to the FAA, there was categorically no physical evidence of any mischief, just a routinely overhauled airplane engine, new propeller, and a phantom car. Nothing to see here folks! Fortunately, no one was injured, or worse, killed, by the otherwise routine buzz job. It's messy and much harder to get rid of a body without someone asking questions. It reminded me of the familiar biplane chase scene in *North by Northwest* with Cary Grant where he had to dive onto the dirt road to avoid being mowed down by the strafing aircraft.

Now, one offense at an unpaid position was one thing; however, I knew that flying was a complex task, and I sought help from the Aircraft Owners and Pilots Association (AOPA). I joined the national organization not only to represent me but as a tool in my flight planning. The best part of belonging to AOPA was the Legal Plan. Because I was human and individuals make mistakes, I needed authoritative advice that was a phone call away. Now I knew if there was even the question of a violation in a complex rule-filled system, I had a resource to fall back on. I discovered early on that the FAA could easily revoke or suspend the license that I had worked so hard to acquire. There was also the NASA form for a one-time forgiveness if you documented your confession soon after the violation, but it did not apply to criminal activities.

Mooney/IFR

The next type of aircraft checkout that I took advantage of was in the Mooney 21 Ranger. The cross-country instrument flight rules (IFR) trip was from Salt Lake City International to South Shore Lake Tahoe and Tahoe, Nevada, to Carmel, California; it was just under six total hours for the round trip. The Mooney was fast, had retractable gear, and was considered a "complex" aircraft. For me, the narrow cockpit was not an issue. South Shore Tahoe presented real thin air issues (referred to as density altitude) in the heat of the day, and I had to study up on the performance of the airplane. To determine if I could safely take off from any remote mountain strip, first I would pace the physical runway to determine the exact midpoint and clearly mark it. If I could accelerate to 70 percent of my takeoff speed, I would continue the departure. However, unable to achieve the predetermined airspeed at the midpoint, I must abort the takeoff, and I would still have time to stop on the runway. Factors such as snow, boggy grass, mud, or standing water all added to the distance needed for takeoff. At airports where the runway was paved (such as Tahoe), it usually wasn't a factor if I took altitude and temperature variables into consideration. I had no idea the doors my new found skills would open for me.

In my logbook on July 17, 1974, I performed my first "hard IFR" departure through a solid cloud deck at Carmel. It was fantastic! As we taxied out, the weather was an overcast, gloomy day in coastal California. I picked up my IFR clearance and departure instructions. After we had been airborne, it was only 30 seconds before we were in the soup and visibility was zero/zero. There was no outside reference, and I had to rely 100 percent on my instruments. Not being able to look outside took discipline for me because I was a new student of flying in the clouds. First, I had to know how to scan the panel and then correctly interpret the instruments, but there was a much deeper commitment that I needed to overcome. I had to implicitly trust what I saw on the instrument panel, knowing that I was traveling well over 120 mph in the clouds. After "cleaning up the aircraft," I turned to the preselected heading and continued the climb at the designated airspeed to my assigned altitude. As I approached the Airway, my Very High-frequency Radio Beacon (VOR) instrument needle centered and I turned on course.

Seven minutes later, I could sense that it was getting very bright outside and that I must be approaching the top of the cloud deck. In an instant, I broke out into the brilliant sunshine. Looking all around, the top layer of the marine clouds were nearly flat. This scene was a most beautiful sight, and I wanted more. Flying IFR gave me a world of flexibility and safety that I had not previously known. Now I understood that this was how an airplane should be utilized.

My first dedicated long night cross-country flight was from Logan, Utah, to Salt Lake City International Airport on August 16, 1974. It was a committing trip, and I was starting to push the envelope. A safe takeoff and departure in the mountainous region required exceptional and detailed planning; I took nothing for granted on the entire trip. I was practicing all of the nighttime cues and tricks that I had learned. I also utilized the IFR skills that I had recently picked up. The "new" environment was daunting for me, but at the same time, I found it to be rewarding and challenging. It heightened my instrument mastery and rounded out my flying skills and confidence. This exercise was a necessary competency and good experience for the qualified pilot, just as mountain flying had enhanced my flatland flying competence.

Flat Spins

In World War II, the Irvin Parachute Company awarded lapel pins to aviators and soldiers whose lives were saved by using their emergency parachutes. It was called a Caterpillar Pin in reference to the silkworm since the early parachutes were made of silk. There were different types of pins in both gold and silver, some with jeweled eyes. A red jewel meant bailing out over enemy territory and green for bailing out over friendly territory."[3] Anyone who documented their aeronautic crisis and applied to the company received the pin, a certificate, and a membership card in the Caterpillar Club. At the end of 1945, there were 34,000 official members. Little did I know but soon I was going to be in a position to make Club application. "Life depends on a silken thread" is the Club's motto.[4]

I piloted a rented Cessna 182 from Salt Lake City to Challis, Idaho, for a Ten-Man Speed Star skydiving competition. It was

---

[3]   The Caterpillar Club, Njaco 09-07-2011 10:57 PM, http://www.ww2aircraft. net/forum/aviation/caterpillar-club-30234.html.

[4]   Caterpillar Club, http://en.wikipedia.org/wiki/Caterpillar_Club.

my most northern mountainous cross-country flight at the time and was very exciting. I was happy to have my friend Terry (Lobo) Loboschefsky along as my copilot and navigator. His presence gave me added confidence, and he was an excellent resource person for me. The weather was fair and the trip uneventful. The well-attended Relative Work (RW) Meet had a smooth start. We were jumping a Beech 18, and the overall conditions were right. The competition was in a sizable valley deep in the tall peaks of central Idaho, along the Salmon River.

The first day of the contest was routine. I even had time to do some local flight-seeing that first evening in the 182. Central Idaho was impressively rugged, and I didn't want to get caught in marginal weather in one of those narrow canyons. Challis was just south of the Lewis and Clark Trail, west of Custer Road, and north of the highest point in Idaho—Borah Peak at 12,662 feet. The small village on the Salmon River was nestled within the Salmon-Challis National Forest, which covered over 4.3 million acres in eastern-central Idaho. Included within the boundaries of the National Forest was 1.3 million acres of the Frank Church—River of No Return Wilderness Area, the largest contiguous wilderness area in the Continental United States. All of this area was encircled by the Bitterroot and Sawtooth National Forests and mountains with names like Corkscrew, Bald, Blue Mountain, and Lone Pine Peak.

Our young, inexperienced jump pilot seemed apt enough the second day until we unwittingly provoked him. The skydiving meet was for speed Ten-man Stars, so there were ten jumpers in the back of the twin-engine aircraft and a single pilot up front. The takeoff and climb to altitude for our second jump of the day were uneventful. During our jump run, the ground crew unexpectedly popped red smoke because they had no radio communication with the pilot. The smoke was to warn us that the wind on the ground was gusting, and it was unsafe to jump using a sports parachute. We made a full orbit, racetrack fashion at altitude, and again started the jump run. Not surprisingly, the winds remained excessively high, and again smoke was thrown as a signal to warn us of the extremely windy and hazardous conditions. Once again, we directed the pilot to continue to orbit, that it was unsafe to jump. On the third pass, the same scenario was repeated. Apparently irritated with us, maybe a bit hungover, low on fuel, or possibly the pilot was on the outs with his girlfriend, he made an uncharacteristically abrupt hard banking left turn to demonstrate his frustration. Possibly, the maneuver was a lame attempt to punish or scare us in some strange and convoluted way. I'm not sure how you scare a skydiver—someone who is fully prepared to jump from a "perfectly good airplane."

Still at 10,000 feet above ground level (AGL), more than 15,000 feet above the level of the ocean (MSL), without warning, the twin-engine aircraft entered a deadly flat spin. A flat spin, by definition, is unrecoverable; the aircraft was clearly out of control. The Twin Beech is a good airplane, but as configured on jump run with most of the jumpers crowded in the extreme tail section of the plane ready to exit, the center of gravity was considerably out of limits in the far aft position in the exceedingly thin (read that unstable) air. The configuration was the lethal scenario for an aviation catastrophe, and the pilot should have been keenly aware of the operational limits of the aircraft and have been following a strict "jump configuration" protocol. If this accident had taken place at a lower altitude or over the nearby mountains, I would not be writing about my aviation adventures.

Our base person, Rolayne Mattsson, was already situated in the open doorway. When the spin initiated, particularly in the tail section, people were instantly pinned in place by the generation of wicked centrifugal forces—a textbook "crack the whip." It was nearly impossible to make any intentional movement due to the severe G-forces. No one had to be told what to do. While we didn't intuitively understand what had just happened, we did know that the Beechcraft was in real trouble, and we were inside the airplane. No one panicked, but we all worked frantically to help each other out of the crippled aircraft. Everyone had the same objective—help move the person in front of you out that door!

With a couple of shoves, Rolayne was the first out, and others quickly followed, one at a painful time. Everyone was straining as if the plane had a case of severe constipation. It was the proverbial emergency bailout against strong G-forces! I was in the very front of the airplane struggling to move to the back as the seconds dragged on. I can vividly recall the event. We were violently rotating in a counterclockwise fashion, and everyone knew we were in dire straits. I couldn't seem to keep track of time, altitude, or rotations because it was all a slow-motion helpless blur. I was anxiously focused on the door and making it out into the slipstream before it was too late. I knew that I had to take my turn, but I had no idea what our vertical speed was although the wrist altimeter on my left arm was in front of my face. All I had to do was look at it. It was scary. But, dammit, I was about to earn my caterpillar pin—just as long as we weren't descending uncontrollably over a nearby mountaintop. In that case, I would not be expecting any minutia whatsoever; I would have already "crossed over to the other side."

Larry Bagley was positioned to be the number ten skydiver out the door, and I observed that he had diverted his attention to the cockpit. Forgoing any possibility of a bailout, Larry committed his efforts to the aircraft controls. Uninvited, he quickly maneuvered into the right seat of the flight deck while the airplane was in an unusual attitude. Bagley was a seasoned pilot and thought it best to put his skills to work recovering from the spin while the remaining jumpers exited to normalize the center of gravity; therefore hopefully making it possible to recover from the spin. While I approached the back door in the number nine position, I thought I felt the centrifugal forces start to lessen somewhat. However, this inkling of reassurance did not impede my advancement nor divert my focus. Honestly, I still had no idea what our altitude was above the local terrain. Time had been obscured, and I had tunnel vision; it was "the fog of war." I looked at my altimeter, but could not focus on numbers; I was only waiting for the impact. As I eventually exited the aircraft, I made sure that I had been thrown clear of the tail section and deployed my canopy immediately without knowing my position, exact altitude, or terrain proximity. It was positively an emergency exit! It might just as well been in the dark over "enemy territory."

At that point, I exhaled, looked down, and checked my altimeter; I was just below 7,000 feet AGL under a splendid square canopy. All around me was high mountainous unforgiving terrain. Fortunately, we were still over the valley that we had been jumping in and not far from Challis and the DZ. I watched the Beechcraft spin away from me in a most detached fashion. I was confident that Larry was going to recover from the violent event. I was the only one on the load who was jumping a ram-air parachute, and I safely landed back on the airfield. Everyone else had round canopies and were at the mercy of the wind and had been strewn about the countryside. They landed in a different zip code, but all were out of "harm's way." The aircraft safely made a pass over the DZ, and Larry jumped to complete the untimely adventure. The wind was no longer a safety factor. I'm not sure if we were charged for that flying circus act, but it didn't count toward the competition.

That night it was Shitty Smitty from Idaho City who kept us all entertained around the keg. We needed more of a distraction than just alcohol to relax the nerves and forget about our close call that day. It was all behind us. The pilot didn't stick around to buy any of us drinks or offer an apology; I guess he was too embarrassed. In the final analysis, we won the competition with four jumps (not including the bailout). Thankfully, the flight home in the rented Skylane was nothing like the one we had just experienced. Unfortunately, we had headwinds and low clouds, but I did not compromise our safety in my rental aircraft. I vowed to learn spins and spin recovery following that practical lesson. It was a real aerodynamic eye-opener for me. I also thought about moving up to the base position so I could be the one in the door and have the best chance to determine my fate.

Cessna T210

With more experience, I set my sights on bigger and more elaborate equipment. The beautiful Centurion that I rented in 1976 was featured on the cover of the Cessna brochure (N2533S) that year. After graduating as a Physician Assistant (PA) in Salt Lake City, I moved to Spanish Fork, Utah. At the nearby Provo airport, I had the opportunity to get checked out and fly a turbocharged Cessna 210. It was very exciting and incredibly fast compared to what I had been flying. Mastering this airplane taught me several facets of aviation, and I learned what it took to fly complex aircraft, which is one with a constant speed propeller, flaps, and retractable gear. The greatest lesson was to be able to "think ahead" of the slippery aircraft and nail the predetermined airspeed. Once you operationally got behind the airplane, if it was going too fast, or it was too high, or you were distracted and made the turn too late, it quickly got ugly.

Flying the Cessna 210 enhanced my flight experience, and I also had five other potential people with me to share the expenses. At that time, it cost me $45 per hour wet, (that means it included gas and oil) for the sophisticated, six passenger, retractable gear aircraft. That rate was still a hefty sum for me, as I was a recent graduate of the Utah PA program, and my wage during PA training had been $240 per month. However, it would soon bump up to $400 after I received my scores from the National Boards. Early flights in the Centurian were to Bullfrog on Lake Powell, Garberville in Northern California, and Mesa, Arizona. I loved the speed and versatility of that airplane.

Pam Budlong and Randy Lippincott in front of the Cessna Centurian T210 he had been flying on the Provo Airfield. Photographer unknown.

Lake Powell trips were always a no-brainer for me. Whenever I go there, I wonder why it has taken me so long to return to this beautiful and mystic land. On this trip, Lobo and I had dates along with a third couple to fill up the six seats in the 210. The trip was straightforward, and we had a wonderful weekend of water skiing and exploring a portion of the extensive Lake Powell shoreline. The journey home wasn't quite as elementary. With a late afternoon departure, we encountered thunderstorms that forced me to make an easterly deviation. The course change took us to Grand Junction, Colorado, before I was able to turn westerly back toward Salt Lake City. I had plenty of fuel to make it to Salt Lake, but the weather in mountainous terrain can be an unexpected factor in your fuel burn. Lesson learned.

The flight to Garberville was first-rate and a fun cross-country for all three couples. The approach and landing at the small uncontrolled field were a bit unorthodox for me. The downwind portion of the pattern was uncomfortably close to rising terrain, and I was happy not to be doing it at night. With a full load at sea level, the T210 was even a more stable and comfortable platform to fly. A limo met us shortly after landing, and our first stop was at a convenience store for a six-pack of Micky's Big Mouth. The party had started! Next stop was a remote hacienda on the 40,000-acre estate well away from the huge wedding crowd. We were guests at an unforgettable and spacious Victorian ranch house that we had all to ourselves. It was beautifully furnished, and I was assigned an upstairs bedroom. We had a Jeep at our disposal, which we used for local exploration. While on foot, I was chased by some very territorial wild turkeys. Yikes, if I only had my shotgun!

It was Lobo and Paula's first date for an over-the-top weekend. The pretense was a large country wedding reception and dinner hosted outdoors with an impressive side of beef barbecued on professionally attended huge open spits and a whole hog slow-cooked in an underground pit. There was no limit to food and drink at the festive rustic cowboy venue.

The two exceptional days were a blur, and I was a bit washed-out when I did my preflight for the return trip. My nighttime departure was by the book, and once the power and cabin lights were adjusted, the climb checklist was completed. On the way home I leveled at 15,500 feet, in the turbo 210, without oxygen, at night—after all, that's how to utilize a turbocharger. Somehow, in my youth, I didn't feel the need to follow all of the rules because the PIC is supposed to be on oxygen when above 12,000 for greater than 30 minutes and continuously when above 15,000 feet. Hypoxia impairs color vision at night, judgment, and reaction time. Lobo and I were able to keep each other occupied, but the four people in the back two rows had succumbed to hypoxia and were sound asleep. The altitude afforded us good radio coverage, a stout tailwind, plenty of ground clearance, and a terrific groundspeed. From that altitude, it was easy to identify the ribbons of interstate highways and distant major cities. Soon, I could pick out the lights of Salt Lake City on the horizon. The utility of this aircraft was without equal in my opinion. Piloting this powerful, complex machine made me feel like a celebrated aviator. It had been a great trip, and I was proud of my accomplishments. Never mind that I was breaking all kinds of nighttime safety rules.

In 1976, I traversed the upper portion of the Grand Canyon (and maybe a little down in the canyon; you know, before all those messy rules were instituted). The flight to Arizona was my first long cross-country trip, and I was flying from Spanish Fork, Utah, in a rented Cessna T210, to a family rendezvous in Mesa, Arizona. My folks and siblings had driven from the Midwest for Christmas at the grandparents, Harvey and Nancy Lippincott. On the return flight, I had the autopilot engaged in the speedy T210 between Flagstaff and the Grand Canyon. I was using the local altimeter setting and flying at the correct cardinal altitude plus 500 feet as prescribed in the VFR hemispheric rules. I could NOT believe it, when from the east (my 1 o'clock position), suddenly and without warning, a Bonanza appeared directly in front of me at my altitude. Someone was asleep at the wheel, and my heart was pounding in my ears. He never even saw me. I was thankful I was by myself, as through my mind flashed the near miss my parents had with a B-52 in Nebraska. There was nothing to do. I was merely an observer. I was amazed that we did not have a 350 mph collision. The Bonanza was going cross-country and should have been 1,000 feet higher or 1,000 feet lower than I was. The FAA rules call for eastbound traffic to fly at odd altitudes plus 500 feet and westbound traffic to fly at even numbered altitudes plus 500 feet. In 1956, the TWA and United midair collision over the Grand Canyon had ignited the air safety controversy and subsequent laws; i.e., the hemispheric rules, the formation of the FAA, modernization of ATC system, and mandated "black boxes" in commercial airliners. Much later, an old timer told me that he always added 100-200 feet to his altitude, to avoid that problem. That advice followed me to Alaska.

The following year I had an opportunity to rent a Piper 180 in North Platte, Nebraska, where I flew out of Lindbergh Field. The airplane was loaded with three other young men for a local flight-seeing tour. At one point I was low-level over I-80 and decided to make a high speed, steep 180 degree turn to impress my friends with my aerobatic prowess. Immediately, I could tell that I had inadvertently entered an accelerated stall half way through the turn. Instinctively, I knew that I had to decrease the backpressure and lower the nose, even though I was already close to the ground. My reflex was to avoid a spontaneous and unrecoverable spin. My youth made me do it, and the "child" gave me the reflexes to correct the near fatal mistake. I could feel what the airplane was trying to tell me. Not one of my passengers sensed the dire straits that we had narrowly escaped. They just knew that their stomachs were suddenly queasy and that sky was out one side of the plane and trees were out the other! *If* the guys in the back seat had been heavier, *if* I had been carrying more fuel, *if* I had banked slightly steeper or pulled back on the wheel just a little harder, it would have been curtains for all of us—one spin and in! The NTSB report would have concluded that the pilot had violated the "stupid rule," and made a stupid, high-G, low-level turn that resulted in an unrecoverable spin. I never pulled that stunt again. Pilots with between 50 and 350 total hours are statistically the most likely to suffer a fatal accident. I was flying directly in the center of the "Killing Zone"—the experience level where low time pilots tend to make the greatest number of fatal mistakes. According to Paul Craig, "None of us can live long enough to learn from every mistake."

PART THREE
Alaska

Alaska, a High-Speed Taxi…

Alaska 1983

The Arctic is replete with crash sites, known and unknown, discovered and yet to be retrieved. The average time for finding an aviation wreck in the land of the midnight sun is well over ten years; some are undiscoverable. There are no accurate figures because we don't know what hasn't been located and how long it was there. The primary factors involved are the vastness of the state and the large number of aircraft flown across Alaska in the 1940s. One of the websites dedicated to those accidents is Abandoned Plane Wrecks of the North http://www.ruudleeuw.com/search116.htm. Maps, photographs, and stories are included in the long history of aviation heartbreak.

During World War II, the Lend-Lease program with Russia provided for 11,400 total aircraft.[5] The Al-Can Highway was built to service the airfields for those planes, most of which were individually flown to Russia through Alaska to be used against the Germans. An incredible 7 percent (almost 800 planes) of those aircraft were lost when the young, inexperienced pilots strayed off course, ran into weather, or had mechanical issues. When I first moved to Alaska in June 1983, the newspaper reported a missing World War II fighter from 1941 had recently been found. At the time of my departure in

---

5   Lend-Lease Shipments: World War II, Section IIIB, Published by Office, Chief of Finance, War Department, 31 December 1946, p. 8. Hardesty 1991, p. 253.

46

November 1993, a civilian plane was discovered outside of Anchorage that had crashed in 1983—the same year I arrived in Alaska. The single-engine airplane had gone undetected for over ten years. The pilot most likely had a stellar aviation career, but it was only the last five minutes that were flawed. In 2015, remains of 17 service members lost in a 1952 military transport crash in Alaska were identified and recovered from a glacier. Snow and ice concealed the tragic event for 63 years. I was living in Alaska on September 1, 1983, when KAL Flight #007 departed from Anchorage and was downed by a Soviet jet fighter after the airliner accidentally entered Soviet airspace (the pilot mis-fed data into the Inertial Navigation System); 269 people perished aboard the Korean Air Lines Boeing 747 including 61 Americans, among them Georgia Representative Larry McDonald.[6] None of those bodies will ever be recovered from the Sea of Japan.

Alaska is an incredible and sometimes inhospitable vast landmass. Adding to the natural remoteness is the absolute lack of roads. There are only a few state highways in Alaska. The terminal portion of the Al-Can Highway, A2, enters from the Canadian border and ends in Fairbanks. The Parks Highway, A3, connects Fairbanks to Anchorage and extends south onto the Kenai Peninsula. The Tok Cutoff, A1, is the hypotenuse of the triangle and is called the Glenn Highway between Tok and Anchorage, and extends all the way to Homer. The Richardson Highway, A4, connects Delta Junction with the port of Valdez. Most of the villages in the "Alaskan Bush" are only accessible by boat (if they are on a river), dogsled or snowmachine (in Alaska there are NO snowmobiles, they are referred to as snowmachines) in the winter, or by air, if they have a runway. There are 403 public-use general aviation airports in Alaska, more than any other state in the United States. The adage in Alaska is, "Fly an hour, or walk a week." Hundreds of rural communities in Alaska cannot otherwise be accessed by the road system. They primarily rely on aviation for their daily survival.

The 49th State boasts the highest peak in North America, Mt. McKinley, or "Denali" as it is now named; and two mountain ranges,

---

6   SFC, 5/29/96, A3. WSJ, 1/23/98, p. A1.

the Brooks and the Alaskan Range. So vast an area, Alaska is the most northern state in the United States, the most western state in the United States—yes more western than Hawaii, and incredibly, it is also the most eastern state in the United States. That's correct, the 1,200 miles long Aleutian Chain crosses the International Date Line. While I lived in Alaska, the summer fire season consumed an average of three million acres of forest per year. These fires were the natural cycle of events, not catastrophic global warming. The majority of forest fires are caused by lightning, but some are man-made, both accidental and otherwise. Wildfires were typically addressed if they were a threat to civilization. These are a few of the extremes found in the boundless Arctic country.

When I first started work at the Tanana Valley Clinic, a secretary learned that I was a pilot. She told me how "experienced" her husband was and said that he was an exceptional and accomplished aviator. Unsolicited, she went on to explain that he had "crashed" airplanes on three different occasions during his career, and those experiences made him a superior pilot. What? I failed to understand her twisted logic or make the same deduction. Is this how insurance actuaries look at things? I don't think so. Had she been a passenger in any of those crashes, her view might have been considerably different. It was the most bizarre reasoning I had ever heard, but apparently, he had her convinced. Oh well, Amelia Earhart had 11 accidents before her disappearance; and she was world renown. During my time in Fairbanks, I read about a midair collision along the Denali Highway (it is a remote gravel road) south of the Alaska Range. The pilots of two Super Cub type aircraft were distracted and circled the same moose east of Cantwell when the unthinkable happened—a fluke mid-air low altitude accident in the Alaskan wilderness. What were the chances? That was just plain bad luck. We will never hear their definitive version of the story.

The Arctic has a well-earned reputation for a high rate of aircraft accidents. Not only do they have the highest per capita ownership of aircraft in the United States, but also the worst safety record. You see, people who live and work in Alaska make an excellent wage and can afford aviation "toys." It is not conducive for those same individuals to fly in the winter due to the extreme weather. All pilots lose skills and proficiency after a period of neglect during the long dark winters. Also, because they tended to be too busy with family to aviate during the summer months, accidents regularly spiked in the spring and fall. Typically, the macho Alaskan has an airplane for moose hunting with his buddies in the autumn. All of this following an intensely busy summer filled with camping, fishing, and boating. Hunting accidents take their toll due to overloaded aircraft and when rusty pilots use poor judgment or cut corners. All of these accidents lead to exceedingly high insurance rates. Like most Alaskan owners, I never bought aircraft insurance for the Skyhawk; they even charged high rates for the modest 172. I could have purchased a new plane in four years with the money that I would have spent on the insurance premiums.

Secondary to pilot inactivity, weather inadvertently plays a role in the aircraft accident rate. Coastal weather brings fog and icing conditions, but frost plays a most insidious role. Once frost forms on the top surface of the wing, it dramatically negates lift characteristics. Hoarfrost must be swept or polished smooth, or else you are dealing with an experimental and unpredictable lifting surface. It is something that cannot be overlooked. A long handled shop broom on high wing aircraft is mandatory or else a crash on takeoff will most likely ensue. It's not just the weather; it is also the lack of real-time weather reporting in the sparsely populated state. Darkness prevails in the Alaskan interior during the winter and increases all the hazards of night flight. Flights in the "Frontier State" tend to be greater distances so fuel management and availability can be critical and real. The list goes on....

The Alaskan pilot is frequently inexperienced and therefore more susceptible to accidents—a fact that is proven time and time again. I was one of those low-time pilots when I arrived. The country is so vast that a pilot becomes accustomed to never seeing another airplane. The absence of encounter is referred to as the "Big Sky" theory and means the sky is really big and it's unlikely that you are going to run into someone else. The majority of midair crashes happen at and near airports for the apparent reasons. In Alaska, pilots often assume that they are the only ones in the air and consequently lower their guard near airports. The majority of midairs are during the daytime in good weather by a faster aircraft overtaking a slower one. A well-known instructor pilot died in a midair collision just south of the Fairbanks International Airport the year following my departure. This deadly scenario is still being repeated to this day.

Early in my career, I took pride in my airmanship. Part of that pride was in my radio discipline; I worked on my verbiage and sentence structure. I grew to detest the thoughtless pilot who didn't think about what he wanted to say until he started to speak. He clogged the frequency with his useless stammering. I wanted to sound professional and act professionally. Since most Alaskan airports are uncontrolled (no control towers), it is incumbent that aircraft landing and taking off make the appropriate announcements on the common traffic airport frequency (CTAF). For me, it was more than proper reporting; it was also astute listening. I would tune in the CTAF to monitor the local traffic as far out as possible. This habit has served me well over the last half century.

I was inspired by Arctic pioneers like Noel Wien, the founder of Wien Air, one of the original brave airmen to tame the Alaskan wilderness. When he arrived in 1924, there were no aviation maps; navigation was only by dead reckoning, and there were few safe landing areas or designated runways. Soon, Wien was making transportation possible where only the dogsled or riverboat had gone before. Wien's story set the hook for me. Adventures were waiting to be discovered on the last frontier.

Your Last Flight Was No Accident—Spin Training

My move to Alaska soon gave me an opportunity to become a partner on a 1983 Cessna 172P Skyhawk. Dr. Richard Raugust purchased a refurbished, nearly new Skyhawk with intentions to acquire his private license. At first, I volunteered to fly with him as a much more experienced safety pilot in the right seat. Soon I was flying the plane more than he was and we became partners. I trained for, and earned, my instrument ticket in this airplane. It was equipped with

World War II era LORAN, which was functional most of the time. Richard and I flew together intermittently for a couple of years. That's when I began teaching myself to spin the airplane from safe altitudes. When confident with my performance, I asked Raugust if he wanted to learn spins. After a single lesson, I guess he had enough. He never flew with me again! I suppose he was just too busy. Shortly after that, he went through a divorce, and as a result, I purchased his share of the entry-level aircraft.

In the Arctic, mechanical equipment needs special attention. The Skyhawk was fitted with wing covers to prevent frost formation and a cowl cover to facilitate preheating the engine compartment. The aircraft was equipped with an 110-volt external plug-in. I used a long heavy twelve-gauge blue extension cord just for this. The blue color signified that it was pliable at 50° below zero. This single connection supplied power to the oil sump contact heater, the firewall circulating hot air heater for the cylinders, and an interior source to plug in an optional cabin heater. The bulky insulated cowl cover was also used to retain valuable heat once the engine was shut down in remote areas. When the aircraft was connected to live power, a small external green light next to the power plug would illuminate. The factory cold weather kit for the 172 included air intake restrictors and an oil cooler cover plate. At such low temperatures, the oil could congeal inside the oil cooler if directly exposed to the extremely cold air. Once blocked, paradoxically, the loss of oil flow would quickly overheat the engine to a critical level. The only other specific Arctic practice was to add glycol to the fuel. This additive prevented gas line freeze if any moisture was present in the fuel. The glycol was more commonly used in the much wetter coastal environment, not the dry interior climate in Fairbanks.

Randy Lippincott secures his Cessna 172 Skyhawk on the ramp in
Fairbanks, Alaska. Photographer unknown.

Cold, dense air improves both the performance of the wing (more
densely packed molecules for increased lift), but also the ability of the
motor to generate increased horsepower due to the higher percentage of
oxygen to burn fuel. It is nature's way of "supercharging" the engine.
In the negative column is the ubiquitous frost, which will drastically
degrade the performance of the lifting surfaces. There is a very real
possibility of icing in the clouds, so pitot heat is frequently used.
The pitot tube has a small hole in it pointing into the "wind," to
detect airspeed. The opening can easily be blocked with ice, so it is
heated. Cold temperatures cause tires to remain stiff, with a flat spot,
if left sitting for any length of time. All fluids are considerably more
viscous at the colder temperatures. Preheating is vital to preserve the
integrity of dissimilar metals and the cranking power of the battery.
An unexpected result of hot brakes occurs when blowing snow strikes
the disc, melts, and then the water refreezes, causing the brake to
lock. Upon landing, the frozen brake, in turn, causes the tire to blow
unexpectedly.

Unless you intend to land in the wilderness, or off airport on
experimental runways, you didn't need expensive skis for your
airplane. Established village airfields in Alaska are snow-packed all
winter and accommodate wheels during the long snowy season. There

is no freeze-thaw cycle with the subsequent formation of ice. Rather, it just snows, becomes compacted and stays there. The hard-packed surface is well consolidated, predictable, and not icy until the spring melt. All "bush runways" were well maintained during the winter months to ensure uninterrupted service to the villages. I only flew into three airfields commercially with concrete or blacktop runways that were plowed clear of snow during the winter season.

Possibly, my scariest incident in Alaska was an innocent flight into the Black Rapids Glacier of the Delta Range on an "ice-cream run." I was unable to get the time off to accompany Randy McGregor and Mark Wumkes on their ski mountaineering trip; so over the weekend, I suggested to Randy's wife that we check on the pair and take them an unexpected treat. We knew about where they planned to travel and could surely find their contrasting tent against the massive white backdrop. Leeann agreed and was positioned in the back seat of the Cessna 172, poised to scan the vast glacier from both sides of the airplane for signs of the mountaineers. Near the surface of the glacier, I was trying to spot ski tracks that would lead us to their camp. Little did I know that I was on a "Highway to the Danger Zone."

That day I made a fundamental error when I continued the search by flying "up-hill," (up the broad and deceptive glacier). As it turned out, I was regrettably flying up a canyon. Because of my distracted focus, I was completely surprised when we were suddenly consumed in a dense fog bank that seemingly came out of nowhere! It was white ahead of us, it was white below us, and it was white behind us! A sense of unexpected mild panic flushed through my body. The situation was a bona fide emergency, and I had to take action, but quick! Okay, I knew what to do. Now I had to act decisively. Survival was a 50-50 chance: Do I turn right or left to avoid nearby rocky obstacles? Could I even remember my location on the glacier? Turning left is the most natural thing for both the plane AND the pilot.

Readers must understand that this is number one on the list of causes of air crash fatalities. It is called flying from Visual Flight Rules into Instrument Meteorologic Conditions, or (VFR) into (IMC). It is unwittingly going from using an outside reference to no visibility from the cockpit for navigation, which results in loss of control during flight. The average survival time is less than three minutes; it takes an average of 178 seconds for spatial disorientation to occur. I did have instrument experience even though I did not have my instrument license. There was no reason to expect that I needed one on this otherwise bright sunny day. The physiology of this condition involves the loss of vestibular senses input or knowing where you are in space. Suddenly, I had to shift from basically letting the plane fly itself to controlling it with only a reference to the instrument panel. That would have been dangerous enough in straight and level flight; I not only had to make the unpracticed instantaneous transition to gauges in the 172 and I had to initiate a turn at the same time. The impromptu change is not without risk of real spatial disorientation or even vertigo. Suddenly I was confronted with a notably high workload and critical split-second decision-making.

Without a word to Leeann (there was simply no time for discussion), I noted my altitude and the reciprocal of my heading. I had tunnel vision for the task at hand. Immediately, I selected 10 degrees of flaps, at the same time pulled the nose of the aircraft up to slow down, and firmly initiated an 180 degree turn to the left. I believed that while adding the flaps, I could help lower the stall speed, and, therefore, tighten the turning radius, make the about-face, and avoid the nearby rocky escarpment that was hidden in the clouds. Shaken by the sudden disorienting loss of any outside reference, I was doing my best to work through the hairy scenario. I would know in a few very long minutes if I made the correct decision or I would come to know only darkness in the remote mountains. There was no time for panic, only action. While in the cold dense clouds, I switched on pitot heat and waited with my hand on the carburetor heat if I should start to lose power. All the while, Leanne remained focused on finding those elusive ski tracks, totally unaware of our predicament. I climbed somewhat and hurried the turn for a faster than standard rate without causing a stall. I stopped the maneuver at my hastily predetermined six o'clock heading. Now all I could do was hold my altitude and wait…. wait for something good to happen or wait for something dreadful to happen. Did I mention how tightly I was gripping the control yoke at that point?

After a few tense minutes, which seemed like an eternity as I felt beads of sweat pop out on my forehead, we emerged back into beautiful blue skies. I let out an audible sigh of relief. Any desire to find the two fearless mountaineers quickly vanished for me, but I did my best to reconnoiter the remaining potential campsites. I never did share with Leanne what had just happened, and she never sensed that anything was wrong. After not finding a trace of the boys, we quietly returned to Fairbanks with the melting ice cream. I had learned a valuable lesson to contemplate, and I started to count my lucky stars. No matter what the mission, first fly the plane!

One of the quirkiest incidents I got into with the 172 was at Gold King Creek, which had a well-maintained gravel runway about twenty minutes south of Fairbanks at the base of the Alaska Range. My friend Larry Mead had a log cabin on a homestead within a five-minute walk of the landing strip. I had flown there many times, and on a lark, one Sunday afternoon I flew out and landed to check on Larry. As it turned out, the springtime runway was deceptively covered in an inviting eight inches of "Styrofoam" snow. It looked innocent enough, but the touchdown was like landing on flypaper. I made a perfect tail-hook "carrier landing," and it was over before I could even react to it. The bizarre snow forced me to use full power for the nearly hopeless taxi to the far end of the runway. The wheels did not float on the snow but rather plowed through the deep and very stiff substance.

I had never seen anything like it. There was no way I was going to take off without clearing the snow by hand. The 172 could not build up enough speed to fly in the unusual conditions. I shoveled the chunky, dense white stuff that day and the next to remove 600 feet of the devil white runway—enough, hopefully, to get up speed for a soft field departure. During the two nights that I stayed with Larry, I read *The Hunt for Red October*. Somehow, I was able to use the airplane's radio to call Fairbanks and have them relay the situation to my wife, Cathy. She, in turn, called my work to explain that I was stranded.

After digging out what I thought should be long enough and wide enough for my departure, I said my farewells to Larry. I started the 172 and let it warm up the oil sufficient to generate full power for my best shot at breaking free of the caked and unpredictable snow. It took almost 15 minutes at idle before all the needles were well in the green. I had drained most of the fuel and gave it to Larry. I only kept what I needed to get back to town; the airplane was as light as it could be for an actual liftoff. The "soft field" takeoff consists of the first notch of flaps, firm back pressure on the control column once I started rolling, and max power. All of this was even feasible in those conditions because I had oversized tires for better flotation on the little Skyhawk. Now, I was about to test that theory and my judgment.

As I started my rollout, the runway didn't seem as wide as it should have been. I tried to focus on the center of my cleared path; but my main gear felt like it oscillated back and forth, catching on the broad, firm snow borders. The parallel berms repeatedly checked my speed as I tried to accelerate. I was thinking, "Why didn't I take the extra time to make a wider runway and should I stop already?" There was no way for me to monitor my airspeed. I had to keep my eyes focused outside on my cleared path and fly the plane strictly by "feel." I needed to do everything by touch, and then I was past the point of no return. I was already committed. Following my initial acceleration, I reefed back on the control column to keep the nose gear from plowing into the consolidated snow at the terminus of my cleared path. In mere seconds, I arrived at the end of the makeshift runway and the moment of truth. It was like taking off in water and hitting a giant wave. The aircraft lurched, slowed somewhat, but continued on top of the "Styrofoam" for an instant. I prayed that the snow's friction would be overcome by the wings' augmented "ground effect." I thought that I sensed a second acceleration, but that could have been wishful thinking. Then, suddenly, I was airborne. Man, I didn't want ever to do that again. I had come as close as possible to rolling my bird into a ball of aluminum! Other than actually being on the ground, there was no way for me to tell that the deceptive snow was an issue for landing or takeoff. Note to self: Next time, "call ahead."

Cessna 205

In 1986, I bought into a partnership with Dave Chaussé on a 1964 Cessna 205. Cole Carson and I each put in $3,000, and Dave put up $6,000. I trained for my commercial ticket with this midsize Cessna while I still owned the 172. I liked to fly the 205 because it was a much heavier and more docile airplane than the 172. For that reason, I chose to practice the necessary exercises regarding the advanced license in the 205. I would rehearse chandelles and the other mandatory maneuvers until I could perform them flawlessly. However, it was in the PA28 R-200 (Piper Arrow) that I took the commercial checkride because it had the retractable gear that the advanced license required.

Dave Chaussé purchased the vintage airplane primarily to service his gold mine at Granite Mountain on the Seward Peninsula. Cole Carson and I volunteered to do the four-hour shuttle to the operation, and over time I flew well over 150 hours to build experience in the wonderful old bird. The diggings located at Quartz Creek were on the north side of Granite Mountain, and, when clear of snow, sported an adequate runway and well-equipped but spartan hut and a large Komatsu backhoe on tracks. It was within sight of a massive decommissioned Distant Early Warning (DEW Line site) over-the-horizon radar, erected during the cold war. Dave tried to land on the rocky mountaintop in his Cessna 206 near the DEW Line station when he wrecked the white and blue workhorse. This crash was the impetus for the partnership in the 205 and my opportunity to fly in the wilds of Alaska. During one of those visits to the gold mine, Dave's partner Mark was charged by a female grizzly bear on the open tundra. Fortunately, he was packing a .44 Magnum. He shot the animal in the mouth at point-blank range, and it ended up at his feet. It doesn't get more exciting than an unprovoked surprise attack by an Alaskan grizzly bear.

Randy Lippincott with a female grizzly bear.
Skinner and photographer are unknown.

Some of my earliest orientation flights with Dave were with our wives. One of those flights with the Chaussés in the Cessna 205 was to Eagle, Alaska. I was gaining skill in flight planning, navigation, and getting the lay of the land. I was learning, on the fly, to solve the problems that the Last Frontier could throw at me. The convenient but narrow downtown Eagle runway was lined with 90-foot tall trees. Approach airspeed was critical, but more important was the realization of the local wind conditions and the real potential for wind shear just as you were landing. The pilot had to note if the winds were favorable before setting up for the dangerous and committing approach. Once the airplane dropped below the 90-foot wind-shadow of the trees, the wing could quickly lose relative airflow and stall near the ground without warning. As the pilot, I had to be able to anticipate these adverse changes in advance and hedge my bets with additional airspeed on short final.

Chaussé was also a private process server and a "repo man." I helped him serve papers and post a property on many a clandestine outing. One tricky flight took place low-level up a river in a heavily wooded mountainous area. At the last possible second, he made a deliberate 90 degree left turn into the trees for the precision landing. At that point, we were well below tree top level preparing to touch down on a surprisingly short strip terminating into a mountain. There was no possibility of a go-around, so everything had to be exactly right the first time. All you had to do was pay attention to the airspeed and skillfully fly the airplane with anticipation. It did help if you had nerves of steel. I learned by observation, and later, with practice, was able to perform at the same level. It did take a certain amount of aggressive risk taking to make the leap of faith and gain the necessary experience. Later, I would fly into many other Alaskan runways that you could only land in one direction and take off in the other.

I Didn't Feel a Thing

On October 18, 1986, Cole and I spent the entire weekend at the Granite Mountain gold mine and delivered a three-wheeler and radio repeater from Buckland in the trusty 205. It was getting late, and we needed to get home to be at work the next day. The weather was marginal, and we started back in low clouds and widespread snow showers. Nearly home after passing Tanana, on the Yukon River, now in the darkness, I was forced to land in Nenana in the thickly falling snow. I was nervous about flying low-level in the dismal visibility and found it prudent to stop short of our destination in the total darkness. I focused very hard on locating the runway in the stormy, mountainous terrain that night to make a safe landing. It had all been by dead reckoning; thankfully, Nenana had a navigation beacon. At last, I spotted the airport lights and set up for a stabilized approach. It was a tense few minutes, and I was unusually anxious to get on the ground. Over the end of the runway, once I had the landing assured, I pulled the power and adjusted the trim to settle onto the heavily snow-covered runway in the no wind conditions. Incredibly, the three point landing was so perfect and cushioned by the thick layer of fluffy snow, that there was clearly NO perceptible way to tell that we were on the actual runway. We just started to slow down in the darkness until I could taxi clear of the runway. After all these years, I have never forgotten that sense of relief and utter perfection extruded from a desperate situation. It does evoke a saying that my instructor used to tell me, "It's better to be on the ground wishing you were in the air than in the air, wishing you were on the ground." We parked the airplane, tied it down, and found a nearby phone. I called Cathy to come and pick us up; she was incensed to have to make the 45-minute drive at night in the inclement weather. It would have only been a ten-minute flight for us in the airplane. I was simply not willing to risk it in the dark and extremely marginal weather!

Decommissioned Granite Mountain DEW Line site on the Seward Peninsula, Alaska. Photographer Randy Lippincott.

I experienced another white-knuckle landing at Nenana in the 205, but this time during daylight hours and in perfect summer weather. My partner, Dave's son Charlie, was with me in the old Cessna. We were returning from Anchorage, directly over the tall, rugged Alaska Range at 12,500 feet, when suddenly and without warning, the airplane started to shake violently. I was sure that a propeller blade had broken off to cause such a brutal vibration. As counterintuitive as it may seem, I immediately throttled back enough over the mountainous region to stop the brutal shaking. Now, gradually, we were beginning to lose precious altitude. The oil pressure was in the green, and there was no oil on the windscreen. The fuel level seemed okay, and I did not smell any smoke. In just a minute, I found the RPM "sweet spot" and was able to nurse it all the way to Nenana as we continually drifted lower. We were nowhere near a road or runway to use as a safety-net. If I were forced to land prematurely, it would be in the mountains or the forest far from civilization, but we made it to Nenana. As a precaution, I made an "overhead approach," that is, I flew over the airfield first and then entered the pattern high enough to land, even if we suddenly lost power. I didn't touch the throttle until I knew I was close enough to the runway to set it down.

Once we landed and shut down, I inspected the propeller; it was perfectly intact! I did a full run-up on the ground, and the engine checked out. I knew something was still fundamentally wrong but didn't know what it was. We cautiously took off again, and I circled to gain plenty of altitude over the airport and then headed towards Fairbanks. We were able to limp into my home field and safely land. Ultimately, the mechanic had to replace an entire cylinder as it had "swallowed" (the valve had broken and was not making a seal for compression) an exhaust valve. All of this, in addition to replacing the rubber engine Lord Mounts that were shredded by the incredibly violent shaking. Later, I discovered that the same mechanic had left tools inside of the engine compartment on more than one occasion. I was not happy. To this day, I still have some of his equipment in my personal toolbox as a vivid reminder.

Some of my favorite and most memorable flights were with my Dad in Alaska. One Sunday we hopped in the 205 and traveled southeast to Quartz Lake for some ice fishing. This lake was a good choice for us because the stiff southerly winds continuously blew the ice free of snow. It was also popular with people who drove their vehicles out on the ice. They tended to cluster near the shore, and it was easy enough for me to land on wheels in the middle of the lake. Before working on the access hole in the ice, I immediately threw a cowl blanket over the engine to retain heat. Dad and I warmed up taking turns running the hand auger through 30 inches of clear lake ice. After several hours, we had a few pan-size beautiful lake trout. I used a sturdy small propane heater (weed burner) and stove pipe that I had with me to direct heat into the engine compartment. At -45° Fahrenheit, the oil was cold enough that I needed to put some hot air on it and the battery before starting. After an uneventful lake departure, we were back in Fairbanks after 20 minutes and had the airplane put away. I cleaned the fish, and we all enjoyed a meal of fresh pan-fried trout. That was the last time I ever took my Dad fishing.

A much more exciting trip, after I started flying commercially, was in the Chieftain low-level down the summertime Yukon River. Dad and I headed to Galena without passengers, so I was able to play a little bit. Flying down the vast and imposing Yukon River low-level demanded all my attention. Dad swore he could see the right propeller raising a waterspout at 175 kts. or 200 mph. Eventually, I had to pull up to make a sharp turn in the river. Prophetically, the name of the bend in the river was the Boneyard. Over time, as the swift water eroded the bank it exposed dinosaur bones for amateur paleontologists. Further downriver, we flew over an open grassy expanse when something caught my attention. Immediately, I pulled up and did the best wing over and 180 degree turn that I could pull off—this time at a slightly higher altitude, I saw what at first looked like a deer, but were two wolves loping through the unusually tall grass. This sight was genuinely wild Alaska. The approach and landing at Ruby caused Father to set up and take notice. The Chieftain was a great airplane, and I felt like I could put it down on a postage stamp. Southwest of Ruby, we overflew the crash site of an old but completely intact Convair F-102 Delta Dagger that had flamed out east of the Galena Airbase during the 1960s. The pilot had ejected safely, and the sturdy aircraft landed gear-up by itself with no significant structural damage. It was a landmark and a shrine to the resilience of man's pursuit of flight.

Cathy's birthday was on January 18th. Unfortunately, each year it seemed that the Valdez Ice Festival was held that same weekend. I was in charge of transporting the Fairbanks ice climbers to the Andy Embic M.D. hostel in Valdez. During the winter, I carried a small propane tank in the external cargo bay (belly pod) of the 205. I used the propane for engine preheat when electricity was not available. While at altitude on one of those trips, the propane started venting into the cabin. I instantly recalled the Apollo 13 explosion; however, I didn't have Houston Control to help me solve the problem. If there had been a spark, short circuit, or a source of static electricity, I would not be here to write this story. Multiple detonations would have ensued, and debris would have rained down over the most remote and inaccessible mountains or glaciers in Alaska. It was a learning experience for me. I can only surmise that I had overfilled the otherwise trusty cylinder because it had never happened before and it never happened again.

The route that I flew to Valdez was the same path that took the life of three young Canadians in a much faster Bellanca Viking. Mark Wumkes and I both worked on the recovery of the bodies amid avalanches in the remote mountains.

The only soul that made the Valdez trip with me, but never returned, was Marti Lewis' dad. She had been my secretary, and after her father had passed away, she asked if I would spread his ashes over the Columbia Glacier on the way to Valdez. This favor was the first time I'd ever been invited to scatter human remains. I tried to think through the technical aspects of the upcoming task to avoid any embarrassment. I was able to negotiate the window, the wind, and the plastic bag of ashes successfully and have repeated the favor since.

That act was at the time of the Exxon Valdez oil spill, and we made a huge triangle flying from Fairbanks to Valdez. I flew over the massive grounded tanker on Bligh Reef and looked down upon the devastating oil spill. Then I turned westerly to complete the second leg of the trip over the vast and scenic Prince William Sound. We briefly stopped for fuel in Anchorage and then flew back to Fairbanks past Mount McKinley. I made sure that Marti only exited the right-hand side of the plane so that she would not notice the fine ash along the left side and tail of the Cessna. It was to be her father's final statement.

One of the handful of willing flights Cathy took with me was to Chena Hot Springs, where we enjoyed a fantastic time soaking in the scalding outside pools when the ambient temperature was a brisk -45° Fahrenheit. The flight made the excursion painless, and the stark contrast in water temperature was amazingly invigorating. During the trip, I climbed to altitude on the direct route from Fairbanks to Chena Hot Springs and was over the White Mountains when my door suddenly "popped open," or more accurately came unlatched, because, of course, the wind forced the door to stay closed. I was inexperienced in that aircraft, but with the sudden sound and pressure change, I was more surprised than I cared to admit. The latch striker plate was beyond repair, and I ended up using duct tape to seal the door closed. The unexpected ruckus did not instill a sense of confidence in my passenger. I believe this may have been one of the last events that bolstered Cathy's loss of desire to fly with me. We never spoke of it afterward.

The next time a door popped open was much later in my career on the Piper Navajo Chieftain. I was in the right seat learning to fly the Navajo when, on takeoff at Galena, the left sided crew door unexpectedly came unlatched. The senior captain was flying the airplane in the left seat and uncharacteristically became totally distracted by the event. I could see that he was preoccupied with holding onto the door, which was entirely unnecessary as the wind would not let it open any further. It was an artificial distraction, and he ignored the fundamental rule of aviation: First fly the airplane. I immediately took over the controls, verified that the gear was still extended, powered back, set approach flaps, and came around in the pattern for an uneventful landing. On the ground, the door was quickly closed, and we finished the day in an anticlimactic fashion. On a different flight, but with the same pilot, the left wing fuel cap flew off. That was another distraction at a critical time during takeoff. I never let anything divert me from the job at hand during any critical phase of flight. There were too many other important things going on to distract my attention when it was so inappropriate.

Gold King Moose Hunting

Abandoned in the Alaska wilderness after shooting, gutting, skinning, and guarding a full-sized bull moose, I nearly became a casualty as a result of profound stress, dehydration, and sepsis. It was the fall of 1986, and moose season was upon us in Fairbanks, Alaska. My hunt had been successful the year before but not as smooth as I had planned. This kill was not going to be any different; Alaska has a way of throwing you a curveball when you are not looking. I flew the Cessna 205 and three of us to Larry Mead's remote cabin at Gold King Creek. Hardly a thirty-minute flight south of Fairbanks, it was the only practical way to travel to the hunting lodge since it was not on a river, there were no roads, and we had to cross lots of tundra. I was the key player in retrieving the large quantities of meat to be harvested.

The well-constructed gravel runway was an easy few hundred yards north of the camp. The setting was a rustic large log cabin, in thick woods with a primitive sod roof and some hand-hewn outbuildings for tools, snowmachine, and a four-wheeler. Larry, the gracious host, willingly chose the lifestyle and lived there full-time by himself. I was not always able to depart that runway as freely as I would have liked.

Cole Carson was a partner in the airplane, Paul Fernholtz was a pharmacist from the clinic where I worked, and his friend whom I will call Russell were all there to moose hunt. I had never met Russell before, but he fancied himself a "bow hunter," and that's what he was going to carry during the rifle moose season. Did I mention that I didn't know him from Adam?

After a big breakfast the next morning, I set out to the southwest by myself and hunted through the tundra and taiga forest for the lion's share of the day. I only wore my army field jacket and carried some power bars and a pint of water along with my Weatherby 30.06. Late that afternoon I ran into Russell, and we decided to hunt together. We headed off in an easterly direction, and just before dusk, I found my target and made a single-shot kill from 75 yards. The big bull moose did not even take one step; the shot was to the heart. Yes, this is how an Alaskan hunt was supposed to go down. I was confident that my nearby hunting partner heard the shot and would show up to help me field dress the mammoth animal. I reloaded my rifle and kept it within reach while I started the task of both gutting and skinning the massive beast. I had to be extremely vigilant after dark because of the threat of grizzly bears. Any bear within miles would be attracted to the enormous and steamy gut pile!

My first moose kill in Alaska had been a spine shot with my .357 pistol at 100 yards. I had to use the handgun because my rifle scope was deformed when I had been struck by a small tree as it was pulled down on me when straddled by the duel wheels on a military style trailer. I was standing on the back of a track rig that we used to pull the heavy trailer through the marsh. It had been a very painful lesson because it hit my head at the same time as it struck the rifle, which was over my shoulder. The tree that bent the steel tube also put a pretty good wallop on the top of my head and knocked me off the back of the skidder. I let out a yell, and the operator stopped before he ran over me. Because the scope was "looking down," the bullet was high, well above its mark. The moose tolerated my first two shots at twenty yards. He hardly paid any attention to me as I continued to empty my gun on him not knowing that all my shots were wild. As the big bull moved away from me, I drew my pistol as a last resort. With a single shot, he went down like I had pulled the rug out from under him. Only after we had him quartered and back at camp did I discover the condition of my weapon.

Now, back to the latest hunt: As I worked into the darkness, no one came to help, but my night vision was more than adequate for the job, and I was content to be endeavoring alone. The gut pile was huge, somewhat difficult to slog around, and a big olfactory welcome mat for any carnivorous predators downwind. I would work on one limb at a time and then one whole side of the animal. Thankfully, I was wearing my dependable knee-high rubber boots, so I didn't worry about getting blood in my socks. I frequently stopped to listen for intruders, sharpen my trusty Buck skinning knife, and note the position of my nearby rifle—just in case. I made steady progress in the remote Alaskan forest. By 9:00 p.m., my work was finished, and I had started a signal fire. As darkness fell on my kill, so did wet snow. I paced myself, but it was a bit tricky to start a fire in wet, snowy conditions. First, I cleared an area to build a fire on top of the snow. Next, I gathered branches on which to build a fire. Then, in a timely fashion, I had to gather dry kindling from deep inside the evergreens. Protected by branches, desiccated dry moss around the tree trunks would be ideal to ignite small green branches, and then the flammable pitch would ignite larger branches for a hospitable fire. The real work was in feeding the flames; it was a continuous effort but did help pass the time. I had no axe, so I was only able to procure small branches and sticks that were quickly consumed by the flames. I had my large hunting knife in my belt, and either had the Weatherby over my shoulder or in my arms each time I thought about *The Saga of Huge Glass.* I loved that thrilling story, but I didn't want to relive his brutal and nearly fatal bear encounter.

Around 10:00 p.m., lights suddenly appeared 200 yards to the southwest. A four-wheeler was headed directly at me bouncing across the tundra. At last, I thought, the signal fire had paid dividends. I directed my attention to the blaze and prepared to welcome my liberator. In minutes I expected to be speaking with my ride, but as I looked back to where the lights had been—nothing. It was as if I had imagined it. How could I have let my guard down? I could have quickly fired a signal shot or, in retrospect, just shot the driver. Did he see my light and was going back for additional help? That didn't make any sense. It took the rest of the night for me to answer that question.

Tired, thirsty, and upset, at about five in the morning, I gave up the vigil and headed back to the cabin. I was more than a little miffed at the night's events and arrived at 7:00 a.m., just as everyone was finishing a hearty breakfast in the dry, warm cabin. No one appeared concerned that I had not returned that night. I guess they would have pulled out all the stops if they had been ready to go home. I didn't know why, but I was not that hungry. I had some coffee, explained the night's events, and told the group where the meat was waiting for them to pick it up. I was not fit to return to the kill site and just wanted to lie down. Suddenly, I felt terribly sick and didn't know why.

Russell did not have a reasonable explanation of why he failed to continue the search and denied making contact when he was 200 yards from my fire. Secretly, I wanted to strangle him. It was unbelievable that he denied seeing my signal flames in the darkness. Why would anyone want to piss off someone carrying a 30.06? Was he blind and stupid? I was livid. I wanted to kick his ass if I only had the energy. It had been twenty-four hours of strenuous work trudging through the tundra and snow with no water, then singlehandedly cleaning and skinning a 1,200-pound moose. Unintentionally, I had pushed the envelope and was feeling the worse for wear.

The day dawned clear, and many hands made light work of quartering and preparing the moose for transport back to town. I was the only hunter to score a kill and was still able to make multiple flights back to Fairbanks with all the meat and passengers. I remember putting the airplane in the hangar and telling my wife Cathy that I did not feel well. I was in no condition to attend the butcher shop ritual that night with my fellow hunters. All I wanted was a bowl of chicken noodle soup and my bed. Later that evening, my temperature soared to 105° Fahrenheit in my withered condition. Ruth Carson and Cathy returned from cutting and wrapping the moose for the freezer and prepared to pack me in an ice bath—yes, it was what I needed. I was miserable, but I tolerated the tub of water FULL of snow and ice with little difficulty. Welcome to the de facto polar bear club. They both sat in the bathroom (I guess as lifeguards if I had a seizure) while I was in the tub as if joking with me bobbing in the field of icebergs was the recommended treatment. My humor wasn't anywhere as high as my temperature. Face it; I was just plain irritable; you would have been too!

After three liters of IV fluid and a CT scan the next day, I was hospitalized for a pelvic phlegmon (a purulent infiltration of local connective tissue). It was all secondary to the severe lack of fluids that my prostate became inflamed, and it spread like wildfire, locally into my pelvis. I was truly septic and would have died if not treated with appropriate strong IV antibiotics. I continued the therapy at home for ten days and made a full recovery. For years afterward, I carried sulfa drugs with me anytime I traveled away from home.

Chronic dehydration was my problem then; now I live in the Arizona desert where everyone is prone to it. I moved from Salt Lake City where the average annual rainfall was 12 inches to Fairbanks, where the total annual precipitation was only 11 inches in 1983. The average rainfall for Phoenix is an even dryer eight inches. My skin yearns for humid air, and I am always mindful that my past medical history makes me more susceptible to a relapse. I still try to focus on my hydration status and my overall general conditioning.

The modern age of the Camelback bladder systems and proper hydration is well accepted. Just go to REI or Big 5 to check out the array of power-drink mixes and electrolyte replacements. The military has also addressed this issue in the Middle East with similar hydration systems. For technical climbing, they have built a hydration bladder into a rack (a shoulder sling that climbing gear is clipped onto) for water while climbing. Today, with a little planning, there is no excuse to deny yourself adequate fluids. The body is up to 75 percent water for a reason. Fluid is essential for even the most basic body functions, right down to the cellular level.

The Quintessential Alaska Weekend

June marks the end of winter and the beginning of summer in the Alaskan Arctic. The sun lazily circles overhead providing urgently needed radiation to the dormant flora and fauna. There is a brief golden period after "breakup" (this Alaskan term designates the coming of spring as ice is swept downstream and melting snow turns into mud) and before the agony of mosquito season when alpine hiking is at its peak. The stable winter weather patterns give way to the more volatile thermal summer skies. "Old Mr. Sol's" arc rises far above his winter path with a proportionate increase in intensity. Well north of the Arctic Circle (an imaginary line, 66° 30' north latitude denoting the northern border of the temperate zone), the sun won't set again until late summer.

In the summer of 1987, Glenn Elison, the Arctic National Wildlife National Refuge (ANWR) manager, suggested an extraordinary "weekend" climbing trip in the Brooks Range. Three of us would fly from Fairbanks to the still frozen Peters Lake. Conveniently landing at the base of Mt. Chamberlin, we could make the round trip in three days. A third local climber was located to complete the group. Mark Wumkes had recently returned from a climbing trip to Mt. Kimball and was in top form. A veteran of Alaskan climbing, Mark had accumulated over 360 total days climbing in the Delta Mountains of the Alaska Range.

As the pilot and co-owner of the vintage Cessna 205, I agonized over the weather for two days as it blocked our attempts to set out on our epic journey. We had allowed for a small window of weather but had intended to use it on location. Although blue skies in Fairbanks summoned us northward, weather reports a mountain range away remained grim. At that point, Glenn canceled due to work constraints. With a half-hearted noon start and every conceivable "Alaskan toy" packed in the airplane, we took off, entertaining alternate plans of soaking frustrated bodies at Circle Hot Springs.

We crossed the White Mountains at 10,500 feet, as the distant silver threads of the Yukon River Basin came into view. Spanning the horizon from east to west, the fifth largest drainage basin in North America unfolded before us. Encouraged by the remarkable visibility, we made a beeline to Fort Yukon for a mandatory fuel stop. The small village at the junction of the Porcupine and Yukon Rivers marks the crossing of the Arctic Circle. Energized by continuous daylight, we pressed on to Arctic Village (typified in Bob Marshall's book *Arctic Village* as, "Houses almost lost in the vast, snow buried expanse of the surrounding country." Ahead of us was the heart of the unspoiled Arctic with its mountains, rivers, and wildlife.

Nestled at the base of the eastern Brooks Range in the Chandelar River Basin, Arctic Village is a quiet sentinel marking the last sign of civilization between the vast interior and a coastal DEW Line outpost. On the Beaufort Sea lies Kaktovik on Barter Island, 127 miles to the north. The isolated Arctic Village of approximately 120 people was accessible only by boat, airplane, snowmachine, or dogsled. Beyond lay the pristine wilderness of the nineteen million acres in ANWR. This park is the timeless Alaskan wilderness at its finest, typified by rugged snow-clad mountains and timeless broad glacial valleys of the Brooks Mountains.

In the ripple free, clear Arctic air at 11,500 feet, we gazed down on fluffy white clouds; lazy captives contrasted with the bold, rough peaks. Able to clearly see our route on the ground, we noted our progress on aeronautical charts. Like virgin tourists, we were awestruck with the splendid and unique scenery that we shared with no one. Noses pressed against the Plexiglas, we strained to memorize each new panorama as it was revealed to us. What an incredible stimulation to the senses! We felt like original explorers of our own "Jurassic Park." The throaty drone of the old Cessna in our ears, the faint smell of oil in our nostrils, and the intense sunshine on our faces added to the mesmerizing effects of the moment. Was the insidious intoxicating effects of hypoxia taking its toll, or were we approaching our very own nirvana?

Ahead of schedule because of tailwinds, we noticed a significant snow-capped peak jutting proudly above any obstructing clouds. We approached it cautiously excited. Yes, It had to be our "Shangri-La." However, our hearts sank at our first views of what appeared to be a large fog bank surrounding the base of Mount Chamberlin. Surprisingly, it turned out to be our sprawling icy runway. With feelings of giddy anxiety, we wondered if this magnificent scene could be ours to embrace and devour. What an absolute prize to discover and behold!

Excitedly, we circled the scenic mountain, wildly snapping photos and making mental notes as we studied our climbing route from our bird's eye view. It would have been nice to have had a digital record to review when we landed. However, as we lost altitude, my personal anxiety climbed. We were descending to land with wheels on a patch of ice 220 miles north of the Arctic Circle during official summer. The gentleman who vouched for the quality of the frozen surface had canceled at the last possible moment. Clear weather and warm sunshine have a relaxing effect unless you are already perspiring. As we flew low-level the length of the lake, subtle irregularities in the ice loomed out at me. My mind raced to explain color changes, questionable texture, and ominous fissures on the foreign white surface. Mark reassured me, "Glenn said the ice was at least four feet thick." I mentally reviewed my "Titanic" evacuation procedures and pulled the throttle back, allowing the reliable bird to settle onto the intrepid runway. A cold hard surface never felt so good, and I started to breathe again. My little gamble had paid off this time. We rolled to a stop in front of the G. William Holmes Research Station and unloaded our gear, acting as though we were pulling into our private driveway after a hard day's work.

Randy Lippincott kissing the solid Peters Lake ice next to the Cessna 205.
Photographer Mark Wumkes.

At 9,020 feet, Mt. Chamberlin is the tallest peak in the Brooks Range of northern Alaska. It nourishes two pint-sized glaciers on its upper slopes. Unlike the massive mountains and rivers of glaciers in the Alaska Range, the Brooks Mountains seem to have been "stunted" by the intense cold of the long winters. Conversely, the perennial snow and ice suffer for only a brief period of the intense "long day" of summer. By the first week of June, there is little snow below the 7,000-foot level. The warm weather has melted all but the thickest ice at lower elevations. Our start from the lake to the summit would span over 6,000 vertical feet—12,000 feet round trip. The climbing route was first ascended in 1960 and is straight forward. The weather remained clear and visibility unrestricted (CAVU). The treeless plain and valleys carpeted in stunning tundra appeared "well groomed," inviting us into its bosom bathed in the soft Arctic pastels of summer.

We quickly selected essential gear only. This outing was to be our "Blitzkrieg" ascent. After a light meal, we shouldered our packs for a short march through the boggy tundra to the base of the climb. As we skirted the lake, we saw overwhelming evidence of the recent migration of the Porcupine caribou herd. Annually, part of the drove of 180,000 passes through this glacial canyon on the way to the Arctic coastal plain and spring calving grounds. New signs of life were abundant everywhere. The remote wildlife refuge is a habitat for musk oxen, grizzly bear, wolves, caribou, moose, and Dall sheep. Further north, the polar bear is a coastal animal as the seal is its main diet. The tundra revealed evidence of new growth and the flora was nourished by sparkling streams and flooded with the enduring daylight. Vibrant smells laced the air, announcing the urgency of the short growing season. The cold, calm, pure air washed our eager faces.

As we gained altitude, the treeless tundra became terraced with huge boulders, punctuated with hearty multi-colored lichen and an occasional bouquet of wildflowers. We stopped to eat and drink; frequently we rested, enticed by the natural tundra bed. Like house cats, we napped as the warm sun circled overhead. Refreshed and encouraged by our steady progress, we pressed on as the slope steepened.

Mark and I reached the halfway point in six hours, including a one-hour nap and rest-stops. At this location, the ridge narrowed, and the firm snow was nearly continuous. Blessed with clear skies and unlimited vistas, we cached all but food, water, and parkas and headed for the summit. We maintained our steady climbing pace around occasional gendarmes and quickly moved over the smooth solid surface. The ridge ahead of us pierced the dark blue sky as if thrust upward by the surrounding gaunt crags.

Water from melting snow causes steep snow slopes to lose their cohesiveness with the underlying rock. Gravity overcomes large snow fields that may spontaneously avalanche due to their mass or be triggered by a man's weight. Soft slab avalanche signs were present on most aspects of nearly every slope, tempering our progress. The imminent hazards were reconfirmed on the steep upper slopes by the ominous hollow sounds we refer to as "whoomps." Enormous areas of consolidated snow collapse from the climber's weight and displace vast amounts of trapped air that causes the unmistakable sound. All of these indications were significant red flags for possible avalanches. Unroped for the sake of speed, we crossed high-danger areas one at a time. Experienced eyes strained for potential slide areas as the stakes increased. The ridge precipitously dropped away 1,500 feet on either side of us! Carefully inching our way upward, we probed with ice axes to test the snow layers for integrity. As we reached the heavily corniced ridge we had named "cake walk," our pace quickened. Now with the peak virtually in front of us, we were halted by a gaping crevasse. Mark discovered a likely place to cross. In melodramatic fashion, we both leaped the gaping abyss, ice axes high overhead, straps flapping in the breeze.

We posed for obligatory summit photos in the calm, clear air; and only then did we realize it was 4:00 a.m. We hollowed out a wilderness perch on the north face of the summit to savor the view. Lawn-chair-style, we nestled in for our second one hour nap, a meniscus of the Arctic Ocean shimmered in the distance. The silent orange disc hovered high overhead shining on our Cheshire cat faces. Now, rested and rehydrated, we started our retreat. Mark and I made the descent in a fraction of the time. Quickly we returned to our cache at the 6,000-foot level, safely retracing our steps.

After feasting on gourmet delights (the chef's favorite was something spicy "South of the Border"), we melted into pre-warmed down sleeping bags; the high morning sun energized our human solar cells. Deprived of rest, relaxing in our nylon cocoons, we sailed off to sleep and were quickly dreaming out of control! The remainder of the descent was expedited by traversing steep scree slopes. Virtually impossible to ascend, we slipped our way to the bottom (skillfully standing up, of course). It was like skiing down the steep rocky slope in our hiking boots and is called glissading.

Like two school boys on a field trip, we tarried; inspecting rocks, watching birds overhead, examining bleached bones, smelling the fragrant Arctic air, and feeling the tundra push back heavy feet. Ever vigilant for the potential grizzly bear, we quickly negotiated the remaining distance along Peters Lake to the Fish and Game cabin and awaiting bunks. The Cessna patiently waited nearby, seemingly happy at our speedy return. Hot brews of cocoa and mocha were poured, and bodies were nourished. As I settled back to relax on the top bunk and play tunes on my Walkman, Mark struck out across the vast expanse of the cobbled white surface on his mountain bike. In the distance he appeared to be a radio controlled model, his fishing pole looked like an antenna poking out of his pack.

Late that evening or early the next morning, I don't recall which, Mark returned with some pretty believable fish tales. The scene was truly Alaskan perfection. The pure calm I found that day would never be forgotten. I did not want to leave. But, as we needed to avoid midday mountain storms, reluctantly we left our magic valley that morning. Clear skies allowed us to retrace our route across the Brooks Range and home unimpeded. Now, 30 years later, I still passionately remember those halcyon days on Peters Lake in the Brooks Range and long to repeat that pilgrimage every June 1st.

Joshua Samuels

I had just proctored the Physician Assistant Boards at the Tanana Valley Clinic in October of 1987. One of the new PA graduates was a gentleman from Sierra Leone by the name of Joshua Samuels. I took an instant liking to him and learned all about his family and life in Africa. As a child, he had picked up raw diamonds out of the stream on their property. His family had lost their factory in the war-torn country, and he had escaped without a hand amputation by the rebels. Joshua immigrated to this country and graduated PA school in North Carolina. Now in Fairbanks, I asked him if there was anything that he wanted to see or do. He said that crossing the Arctic Circle was his greatest desire. That hour and 15-minute flight to Fort Yukon in the 205 would cement our life-long friendship. Fort Yukon is eight miles north of the Arctic Circle at the confluence of the Yukon and Porcupine Rivers. Once we had landed in Fort Yukon, Joshua could check that off his bucket list.

My next visit with Joshua was in New York City at the National PA Convention. The opening event was a "Night in the 60s" dance, and 500 people were on the dance floor. From out of the crowd, I heard a "Raaandee, Raandee!" Yes, it was my friend Joshua. It was an unexpected and welcomed reunion. Years later he retired from a clinic position in Nome, Alaska.

Joshua Samuels in New York City. Photographer Randy Lippincott.

The Skyhawk Is a Migratory Bird

My first truly long cross-country flight was in 1987, from Fairbanks, Alaska, to Las Vegas, Nevada, via the Grand Canyon and Salt Lake City on the return portion. Round trip by car it would have been over 7,000 miles. While moose hunting, I had observed the beautiful fall migration of the familiar Sand Hill Crane winging their way over the Alaskan Range. The crane from my home state of Nebraska flies 5,000 miles one way to Eastern Siberia on their annual migration. Cranes have been around for 60 million years, one of the longest successful spans of any animal on earth. It is the oldest living bird species' and has been virtually unchanged for the last nine million years. As I put it all into perspective, my trip didn't seem so daunting.

Mark Wumkes and I planned to attend the November 1987 American Alpine Club annual meeting in Las Vegas. It was about a 26-hour flight both ways, and it would be one of the several times that I would fly the Canadian "trench" in the Skyhawk. That first day we landed in Whitehorse and camped under the wing of the airplane in -45° Fahrenheit temperature. We were able to plug in the little airplane on the ramp and walk across the street to a nice restaurant. I enjoyed having Mark as my navigator and "chief mechanic." The days were short, and we did most of our flying in the dark while in the Arctic backcountry.

I carried extra fuel in the cabin and only on one occasion during the cross-country trip did I have to make an impromptu landing at an otherwise unnamed, unlighted, remote airstrip to add fuel to my tanks. It was in the middle of nowhere along the "trench" in the twilight. This valley was a vast and long north-south geologic formation occupied by Williston Lake. Even in the fading light, we were witness to expansive checkerboard clear cut activity. Closer to civilization the smell of the pulp mills wafted through the cabin. The picturesque town of MacKenzie was our day's destination at the southern tip. Other fascinating Canadian stops included Kamloops, Quesnel, and Prince George. We processed through customs in Oroville, Washington.

We had several memorable incidents during that first long trip. After we had crossed the Canadian border into Washington, we spent

---

7   https://www.uhaul.com/SuperGraphics/59/2/Venture-Across-America-and-Canada-Modern/Mississippi/Oldest-bird-in-the-world

the night at The Dalles in the Columbia River Gorge. In marginal weather, we took off early the following morning. As we flew low level, scud running (that is flying near the rugged ground, dodging the clouds), I was focused on my route. Looking forward, I needed a split-second response time to avoid rising terrain, power lines, or radio towers that might appear out of the mist. I had no clue that a Navy A-6 Intruder was painting us with its radar. Apparently, he was out for a little fun by himself, and he spotted the 172 as a suitable target on his screen. Without warning, he dove on my little Skyhawk from behind and filled the windscreen with his Navy jet. It surprised us more than you can imagine. In an instant, he disappeared into the clouds, and we were awash with the blast and sound of an accelerating jet. JEEEZE, once I caught my breath and righted the aircraft, we were both giddy with amazement following the unbelievably close encounter. My adrenaline was through the roof! Of course, in hindsight, it was all great fun, and it did not matter that our hearts had stopped for a few protracted and debilitating seconds. If I had been in the jet, I would have done the same thing.

In Northern California, we ran into unforecast stiff headwinds. Low level, we tried to get under the wind; it was depressing to look down on cars and trucks on the freeway going faster than we were. This predicament caused me to make an unscheduled stop for fuel. Somehow at the time of my run-up before takeoff, I failed to switch the mags back to the BOTH position. We were able to take off with moderate density altitude (increase in density altitude decreases aircraft performance), but the airplane failed to accelerate in the "single mag" position. Immediately, I sensed that something was very wrong, and I quickly returned to land. My mood turned from a bit sheepish to relief when I discovered that my only problem was the position of the ignition key. The NTSB report would have read, "pilot error," and "Mr. and Mrs. Lippincott, we regret to inform you that your son was acting foolish and demonstrated improper use of the airplane key and two people are dead because of it."

Long before the days of cell phones, I called back to Fairbanks every few days to check in. Cathy liked to remind me that Paul Newman called his wife Joanne "every night" that he was away. To add to my wife's consternation, she described a local Cessna 185 that had gone missing the day of our departure. Moose hunters were coming back from Ruby, Alaska, and called into the Control Tower 10 miles southwest of Fairbanks in preparation to land. Mysteriously, they vanished off the radar without a distress call or an emergency locater transponder (ELT) signal. They didn't make it home and were never heard from again. In fact, the crash site was not found until several months later, well after we were home. The NTSB concluded that a tent pole in the tail of the aircraft had jammed the controls and caused the fully loaded ski-equipped Cessna to go into an uncontrolled spontaneous nosedive. The decidedly small vertical impact zone in the tall trees and complete lack of fire left the fateful crash site undetectable even by air. There were no other signs at the time of impact, only a small crater in the frozen forest. The tragic accident that took four souls occurred in the vast Rosie Creek area, the site of a forest fire that was burning the day I first arrived in Fairbanks during June 1983. It was where I harvested my personal annual supply of firewood each year.

Following the Las Vegas meeting, and a moderate local climb with the rising rock star Lynn Hill, we traversed the vast Grand Canyon and flew on to Salt Lake City. The trip took us from the cold Arctic to the warm Southwest, and then we were headed back into the Arctic. Our last overnight in Canada was at Fort Nelson on the Al-Can Highway. Upon departure, westbound, the otherwise reliable 172 uncharacteristically sputtered on rotation. This sudden event took my breath away, but in a few seconds, it passed without any input from me. Somehow, I didn't find it necessary to return to the airport to investigate the transient issue. Once we safely returned to Fairbanks, the aircraft went for a routine inspection. The mechanic later asked me how we could fly the airplane with so much water in the fuel. As it turned out, the main sump was entirely full of water. My very dim light came on. How could I have let something so basic as that happen on such a critical trip? I had been very lucky that the sputter hadn't turned into deadly silence. With the change of temperature, coming from Arizona to the Arctic, water had condensed out of the humid air and contaminated the fuel.

A Needle in My Soup

After my initial exposure to the IFR environment in a Mooney on the California coast, I wanted to learn all the skills necessary for instrument flight. Now, after acquiring my instrument ticket in the 172, I was anxious to put it into service. Ruth Carson had a long distance meeting in Tok, Alaska. She agreed that the trip would be much easier if we flew versus her driving the very long distance. In August 1989, I scheduled the time and filed an IFR flight plan to Tok on the airway. The weather was slightly better than marginal, and everything was uneventful until I passed Delta Junction. Then for some reason, while in the soup, I transposed the heading numbers on the outbound course. Now, instead of traveling southeast, I was headed south directly into tall mountains. Only a few minutes past the navigational aid, Anchorage Center raised me on the radio and asked me to verify my heading. Immediately, I understood my error. I was grossly diverging from the planned airway, into the region of high terrain, and was soon back on course in the clouds with a centered needle on my VOR and back on the planned airway.

After we safely arrived in Tok, I waited patiently for Ruth to complete her therapy session and had already filed a return IFR flight plan to Fairbanks. Now the overcast was thick, and most of our trip would be in IMC conditions; i.e., we were in the clouds. The ceiling was low, and immediately after departure, we were in the very cold, moist solid overcast. On climb-out, I quickly sensed that we were losing power and unable to continue our meager ascent. Did I sleep through the class when they taught about this scenario? There was no ice on the windshield, no ice formation on the struts or the leading edge of the wings. Now comes the actual test of the young aviator: fly the airplane, stay on course this time, and mentally troubleshoot the problem. I deduced that it could only be one other thing—carburetor icing. Slowly but deliberately I initiated carburetor heat. Water sucked into the engine caused a bit of a sputter when the carburetor ice started to melt. Worrisome at first, now I activated full carburetor heat with a resultant dramatic increase in power. Wow, I didn't see that coming! Although I completed that flight safely, I never really knew if Ruth had doubts in her mind about my aviation skills, and she was too polite to say anything to me.

My absolute favorite "local flight" was to the extremely rugged and scenic Debra, Hess, and Hayes tour in the Alaska Range south of Fairbanks. These mountains are striking, esthetic, and impressive snow clad peaks. They're majestic silhouettes but even more magnificent up close, on foot or from the airplane. When conditions were perfect, it was a beautifully jaw-dropping adventure. I could get a sense of the local conditions when flying very close to the tall remote mountains. Debra and Hess shared a high altitude, exquisite, but extremely narrow and imposing saddle between them. In geomorphology, this is referred to as a "col" and is the lowest point on a mountain ridge between two peaks. To cruise along the north face of Debra and slip through the pass at a committing 45 degree angle was only slightly risky, but it was seriously close and intimidating quarters to the uninitiated. It was more than awesome; it was just plain overwhelming. It was truly a once-in-a-lifetime experience and akin to being in an interactive IMAX movie. I needed to know that I was flying in perfect conditions before I would consider "threading the needle." The proximity of the towering, massive granite peaks above the endless sweeping expanses of crevassed glaciers would cause anyone to take a deep breath, or in one instance a macho passenger puked into his telephoto lens case. The sheer vastness of these massive, godforsaken, and wild mountains was overwhelming, even to the most seasoned Alaska Range aviator.

Rich Anderson M.D. loved to fly with me. He was a gynecologist who worked at the Tanana Valley Clinic while I was there. When not scouting the fantastic Alaska Range, or "threading the needle," we traveled to Dawson, Yukon Territory, for an entertaining weekend. He was interested in aviation, and his involvement was infectious. Rich loved to see the Alaskan wilderness from above! I took him along with his mother and sister to view the wild Black Rapids Glacier and hunt for Moulins (a hole in the glacier, part of its natural plumbing).[8] We traveled to Chena Hot Springs, Tanana, Minto Flats, McKinley Park,

---

[8] http://en.wikipedia.org/wiki/Moulin_(geology)

Mt. Debra, Hess, and Hayes, and he flew as my safety pilot for many practice instrument approaches in the 172.

A Moulin exit ice cave in the Black Rapids Glacier, Alaska.
Photographer Randy Lippincott.

Another physician whom I enjoyed traveling with was Jim Fuzzard, a radiologist from Fairbanks. His blue and yellow Cessna 170 was a labor of love. Jim had his 170 on floats in the summer and wheel-skis in the winter. I learned a lot by flying with him. I grasped the ramifications of glassy water landings and learned that the only way to approach them was to set up a 200-300 feet per minute rate of descent on final and NOT anticipate touchdown. Glassy water landings are well known for the loss of depth perception and flaring too high with catastrophic results. The floatplane must be flown onto the surface under power. I discovered that you could land anywhere on floats; it's the taking off again that can be problematic. Part of the expanded checklist was to sump your floats; that is, make sure that you didn't try to take off when they were full of water—it just wouldn't work.

Floats opened up a whole new world of exploration. Alaska has over three million lakes greater than 20 acres in size. These lakes may afford hunting, fishing, camping, or even cabin access. Rivers required an entirely different mindset. First, depending on the size and speed of the current, a sufficiently long and straight enough area must be located to land AND take off. The area was evaluated to plan an upstream landing and then safely take off downstream and still be able to avoid nearby trees or terrain. Oh yeah, overflying the area to check for logs, stumps, or sweepers was always a good idea. A resultant hole in a float would mean a one-way trip in the wilderness and a long hike out.

Skis were utility items with special rules. Hydraulically, you would pump the skis down for a snow landing and pump them up, to expose the wheels, for a runway landing. The pilot had to be aware of the type and quality of snow, often a "touchdown" short of landing was required. That is, we would drag the skis on the snow surface to get a "feel of the snow," the length of the proposed runway, and take off again. Then a subsequently committed landing would be on the same tracks for predictability. At the end of the runout, we would make a U-turn pointing in the direction of the anticipated takeoff. Depending on the intensity of the sun and outside temperature, the skis could freeze on the disturbed snow. We would rock the wings or use the tail as leverage and free the skis before attempting any departure. The ski-equipped airplane made an infinite number of landing areas possible.

Dr. Jim Fuzzard with his Cessna 170 on floats.
Photographer Randy Lippincott.

After my successful summit bid on Mount McKinley in May 1984, I loved revisiting the now familiar massif with a full circumnavigation in the 172 on New Year's Day. The routine was to make the trip in a counterclockwise fashion, and it soon became a tradition. Coming from the north, I headed toward the avalanche-prone and forbidding Wickersham Wall, then continued to climb until I could safely navigate through Denali Pass. In the notably cold air (-45° Fahrenheit), the normally aspirated 172 could maintain 14,000 feet, well above its regular summertime service ceiling, around the huge mountain. I loved to revisit the West Buttress (the route that I had ascended) and scout out the imposing south face of Mt. McKinley along with the expanse of surrounding world-class mountains and glaciers. Impressively, these included the Ruth Amphitheater, the home of the Sheldon Mountain House; the Great Gorge of the Ruth Glacier with mile high granite walls filled with a 4,000-foot deep river of ice, and the deepest canyon in North America. It was bordered by one of the areas' great climbing walls called the Moose's Tooth. The longest glacier feed by McKinley was the Kahiltna, which stretched 44 miles south toward the Pacific Ocean. Famous neighboring mountains were Mt. Foraker to the west, and Mt. Hunter and Huntington to the south. The list of mountains and climbing routes goes on and on. Each was considered world class and committing.

On one memorable trip along the north side of the Alaskan front range, I was flying solo eastbound just above the tree-tops when I surprised a wolf pack attacking a full grown moose. The adult cow, taken to her knees in a clearing, had almost made it across a shallow river. With my unlimited view and front-row seat, I counted eight wolves in the pack. They were slashing her hindquarters, back, and face. They gave me no notice whatsoever. I quickly established slow-flight and circled the incredible primal sight until I could confirm the final results. The huge animal had been singled out, ran until fatigued, and then worn down by the organized, vicious, wild pack in the open wilderness. I couldn't help but recall the words of D.H. Lawrence, "I never saw a wild thing sorry for itself." I was witness to nature's real time, "circle of life," and it evoked certain primordial feelings deep within me.

Most of Alaska is only accessible by air and Manokotak is one of those places. On this trip, I had agreed to pick up Joan Walser in Manokotak on the Igushik River in southwestern Alaska. She had finished teaching school for the year in the small native fishing village that was at the very southern tip of the Wood Tikchik Lakes. It was a great journey for me through the incredibly rugged and intimidating Lake Clark Pass—a truly wild and scenic mountainous area and home of several active volcanoes. Joan had a carrier for her canine buddy and a small overnight bag; otherwise, she had already shipped everything to Fairbanks. Her dog was a perfect little passenger and didn't bark once on the long four-plus hour flight home. Our return route traversed the well-known Lake Iliamna, Anchorage, and Mt. McKinley. Usually, on long north/south trips, I flew within sight of the Parks Highway, I never knew when I might need an emergency landing strip.

Wind Shear

I unexpectedly experienced my first verifiable wind shear during nightfall in Wasilla, Alaska, February 1, 1989. Doctor Charlie and Cindy Steiner and Randy McGregor MD accompanied me to an avalanche mountaineering course in Hatcher Pass. At the end of a long and exciting weekend, we loaded our skis and gear and piled into the 205 to head back to Fairbanks. We were not overloaded, had adequate fuel, and the run-up in the dark was normal. Shortly after rotation, and at an altitude of about 50 feet, during the most critical stage of flight, the wind did an abrupt 180 degree shift. Suddenly, instead of climbing out at a controllable 80 mph, my airspeed had dropped to a very critical 65 mph, and the airplane started to settle back to earth and into the dark and forbidding forest. It was more than just a sinking feeling; it was indeed happening. The controls instantly became "sloppy," and I could tell that something was seriously wrong. Spontaneously and contrary to all my instincts, I lowered the nose toward the foreboding treetops directly ahead of me. Little beads of sweat broke out on my upper lip, and I applied a death grip to the control yoke. I was able to eke out just enough airspeed in time to prevent a stall, avoid the treetops, and accelerate enough to regain control. Inattention in the darkness, an overloaded airplane, a moment's distraction, or just plain bad luck would have ended in an off-airport landing in the nearby forest. I never wanted to experience wind shear on takeoff again. It was a horrible, gut-wrenching, and utterly helpless feeling. The visual was even worse, huge dark pine trees surging up out of the darkness intending to interrupt my flight.

Takeoff is one of the critical phases of flight for a good reason. It demands 100 percent of the pilot's attention even if nothing untoward happens. The aircraft accelerates from zero mph to the minimum airspeed at which it can fly. Slow flight is somewhat facilitated when the aircraft is less than a wingspan above the ground. The wing is effectively able to push against the runway for additional lift. This advantage is called "ground effect." Once higher than the wing span, the benefit of ground effect goes away. At that exact critical level, the wind shear is the most deadly, causing the wing to stall. At that point, the aircraft is too low to recover, and the result is a crash landing. The other critical stages of flight that demand complete attention are landings, climb-outs, and descents. The only phase that is not critical is cruise flight. As the pilot, at your predetermined altitude and power settings, you can be more relaxed at the controls in straight and level flight.

The voyage home after the marginal takeoff was uneventful. No one realized that the flight had been in question and they were all relaxing in a slumber state on the return trip. Charlie didn't understand, "You have instruments in the plane, what could go wrong crossing the Alaska Range at night?" He did not have all the details to understand the IFR rules. The problem was that the minimum enroute altitude was higher than the operating ability of the old Cessna 205. Confirmation of the close call was made in Fairbanks hours later when I put the airplane away that night; a collection of pine needles around the right brake pad told "the rest of the story."

Dipnetting Chitna

East of Chitna, Alaska is a scenic and historical hard rock digging called the McCarthy-Kennecott Mine. No longer operational, the McCarthy site was an underground copper mine. Today it remains as a vast old superstructure that is the attraction to the area. It is a unique sight from the air when it suddenly appears, isolated, out of the vast Alaskan wilderness.

Not far west of McCarthy, in Chitna, on the mighty and swift Copper River was my favorite place to fish and one of the most productive ventures with the Cessna 205. After removing all four of the rear seats, the large cabin could easily accommodate six large ice chests. I would fly southeast through Isabel Pass, the same route where the support team had stopped the day before to pack the bulky Styrofoam chests full of snow. For them, it was 300 miles and an 8-hour drive to the Copper River. My flight was less than 2.5 hours each way through the panoramic Alaska Range. One fisherman would trailer the power boat and dipnets to the river and then pick me up once I landed on the gravel strip in nearby Chitna.

The harvest routine was as follows: Two or three of us would motor upstream and then drift with the current along the banks of the Copper River. All the while we would have one or two nets in the water bumping along on the river bottom. The nylon net was secured to a two-foot aluminum loop at the end of a ten-foot pole. King Salmon swim upstream along the sides of the river where the current is not as swift. Once the enormous fish swam into the net, all I had to do was reef it in and deliver my trophy onto the floor of the waiting boat. After about three or four 35-45 pound salmon had been secured in the vessel, we would head back to the beach where the cleaning crew would gut and pack them in the snow filled coolers.

By midday, we had our limit; the coolers were full, and I would fly the fresh salmon back to Fairbanks for processing. A small team would spread the trophies out on tables in the driveway, where we would expertly cut the salmon into filets and steaks, then vacuum pack them for the season. They were then divided amongst the participating families. Throughout my years in Alaska, I always had three things in my freezer: salmon, halibut, and moose meat; smoking them was an option year-round.

Randy Lippincott processing King Salmon on the Copper River.
Photographer unknown.

On these trips, I sometimes let one of our vehicles get well ahead of me on the highway before I departed Chitna. After giving them some lead time, I took off with the intention of spotting their automobile on the road. It did not take much practice to drop out of altitude and at about 150 mph swoop the car from behind. The driver of the car never saw it coming, even if he was expecting it. First, the plane would fill the windscreen and almost simultaneously they were hit with the distracting roar of the air-cooled Continental 0-470. It was a jolt even for the most focused motorist. The vintage 205 was orange and white, so it even looked like the blur of a salmon in swift waters. After all, we called it the salmon run!

Ryan Air—Ice Fog & Parker Brothers Monopoly

Working as a full-time pilot in Alaska continues to be a risky occupation. During 1990-2009, aviation crashes in Alaska caused 149 occupational pilot deaths (does not include military), an average of eight pilot fatalities per year. These 149 casualties over 19 years were from a commercial pilot workforce of approximately 2,600[9] or over 17 percent of the workforce. A gruesome rate of attrition.

One of the most difficult times I experienced as an adult was moving away from my family in Fairbanks to fly on the west coast of Alaska in the winter of 1989-90. I left my established career in medicine for an unchartered occupation in aviation. During my mid-life crisis, I attempted to transition to a lifelong love of flying. In the end, it was an incredible but costly experience. I became familiar with many fantastic and spectacular places in Alaska that others may only experience in pictures. Unfortunately, it also put considerable stress on my marriage.

My Alaska experience started in earnest during the winter of 1989-90 on the Bering Sea (90 miles north of the Arctic Circle) in a Cessna 207. They were all painted red, and we called them "sleds." The SR-71 Blackbird spy plane is also referred to as a "sled" by its drivers. However, our sleds would never go 2,000 mph or exceed 85,000 feet, but I landed mine in places every day that they would never even consider. The 207 was a seven-seat, single engine piston workhorse. It was a great utility airplane, and weight and balance were always an issue to be considered on every takeoff. The long aircraft had no deicing equipment on it, and it was NOT certified for flight into known icing conditions.

The company route system for Ryan Air was laid out for VFR only aircraft because we flew single engine equipment. A twin-engine plane was required by the FAA to fly passengers IFR. Moreover, although Kotzebue did have an instrument approach, none of the destination airports were equipped for instrument procedures. A few of the villages had radio beacons allowing us to use our automatic direction finders

---

[9]   http://www.cdc.gov/niosh/topics/aviation/.

(ADF). Most non-pilots do not understand the complexity of IFR or instrument operations. To fly IFR in the system, you must be rated, your aircraft and airport must be equipped, and you need radio and usually radar contact with Air Traffic Control (ATC or referred to as "Center"). The controller must approve your route, spacing, approach, and be able to guarantee separation from other aircraft. None of this was feasible for remote village travel. Our low-level routes were never in radar coverage, seldom in radio contact, and we did not fly twin-engine aircraft. What we had to work with were slow, single engine, non-de-ice equipped, old airplanes. Although there was snow everywhere, we never used ski-equipped planes. The runways were typically hard packed snow, and we only flew on wheels. Occasionally our brakes would freeze, but I never put myself in the position to get stuck in deep snow or run off the runway.

Dale Merle Walters was the no-frills station manager with Ryan Air who gave me my big break. Known as the "Arctic Grouch," Dale helped me survive those critical and stressful times, that first winter north of the Arctic Circle. As the chief pilot in Kotzebue, Dale drew on his 50 years of combat and civilian aviation experience in his daily operations. I looked up to Dale and knew that he would test me in more ways than I could imagine. It was an initiation that everyone did not survive in that harsh and desolate environment.

Walters may have seemed surly at first glance, but he ran a tight ship and cared about his employees. I immediately liked him and appreciated his dry wit and practical thought process. He was willing to share his vast flying knowledge with wet-behind-the-ear pilots like me. His military career included flying the Stearman, AT-6, P-40, and P-51 warbirds. Although reluctantly, he also told the stories of two tours of duty in P40 Warhawks and then P51 Mustangs against the Nazis. I was in the presence of an authentic World War II unsung hero (yes, the Greatest Generation). He told me that he had been shot down behind German lines, but was a survivor and had lived the "Great Escape," not once, but twice.

Information only released in 1985 detailed the secret tool used to facilitate the escape of 35,000 Allied POWs. The Parker Brothers Monopoly Game had a significant role in those breakouts. The

British took over production of the popular game that shipped in Red Cross boxes to targeted POWs. An established code used in outgoing "innocent letters" let British Intelligence identify the "Camp Escape Officer." The specially modified game was shipped to that officer because he was the only one knowledgeable of and privy in its use. The game board was tagged with an inconspicuous small red dot in the "Get Out of Jail Free" corner. At that point, the POW knew that there was real German money (Marks) stashed within the play money, that a small disguised compass was one of the game pieces, and that the physical board contained a silk map to guide the POW through the local enemy territory. The cloth map was the key component and essential for a safe return to friendly lines. I acquired one of those coveted silk maps from the Army Surplus Store as a kid growing up.

During my training with Ryan Air, I stayed in the "apartment" above the company hanger with a Russian refugee by the name of Boris Grachov. We slept on the floor and only had one table with two chairs. He was a hulk of a man at 6' 6", and did an excellent job as a freight handler with his powerful giant hands. The Russian was mild-mannered, and we got along splendidly. Boris had a very colorful background and didn't mind talking about it in his thick "Saturday Night Live" like Russian accent. Boris's stories helped while away the long hours of the dark and cold winter nights. During one particularly slow evening, I occupied the time by cutting his extremely long and unruly black matted hair and beard. I don't remember it being much of an improvement when I was finished, just shorter. Boris didn't seem to mind the attention, and I realized that my career as a hairdresser was short lived.

Initial Operating Experience (IOE) is learning how a business operates and getting used to the company trips; IOE falls under the purview of company training. If a check airman has a line or route, training can displace the scheduled captain and substitute the IOE candidate as needed. If the check airman was not required for IOE that month and had no duties in the simulator or elsewhere, then he could fly as a regular line pilot. Along with the orientation, came learning the parameters for making a Go/No-Go decision for each flight. The dispatcher was going to make that decision for you because she had all the up-to-date information from the village and other pilots. All you could do was turn around once enroute if the conditions had changed drastically; that is, unforecast icing, zero visibility, or a medical emergency onboard. The dispatcher would have already called the village and received real-time weather information. Our agent on the other end understood weather and travel stipulations. After all, it was a neighbor or likely a family member on that flight, so everyone had a vested interest.

I never turned down a trip but did return to base without landing at my destination on one occasion during my career. It was at the remote and extreme northwestern point of the Alaskan Coast on the Chukchi Sea in clear weather. The Cape Lisburne runway paralleled the water's edge at the base of a large mountain and was 90 degrees to the typical downdrafts or a sudden and deadly williwaw. On the first attempted landing, I found it prudent to "go around." After multiple approaches to the runway, I was unable to come close to landing due to powerful and unpredictable downdrafts. Like so many other landing strips in Alaska, there was no point in risking everything on a well-known treacherous airfield. I realized that this was not the typical crosswind landing, but rather, a crap shoot on whether I would be hit by a strong downdraft just as I was trying to touch down—like wind shear on steroids.

There was very little daylight north of the Arctic Circle in the winter. It was cold, dark, frequently snowed, and airframe icing was always possible. I chose to work in that environment, so I didn't miss the sun while it was snowing. Empirically, I knew that it was still there, it's just that I couldn't see it. It may sound eccentric, but I did love it; all one needed to do was dress appropriately. Essentially, every day was a challenge and hard work. It was as much mental as it was physical. Company training seemed to occur around the clock or at least during my waking hours. My job started in the dark and finished at the end of a long day under the same cloak of darkness. Between 10:00 a.m. and 2:00 p.m., it was light enough to read a newspaper outdoors, and then later in the season there was actual reassuring direct sunlight on the horizon. I knew that next summer, I would experience 24 hours of daylight. During the change, at some point, I was either losing 8 minutes of daylight or gaining 8 minutes of daylight every day. The joke was, "What do you do during the day (daylight time) in the Arctic? Answer: Have lunch."

My company training in Kotzebue took nearly two months, and I logged over 70 hours in the Cessna 207. Warren Thompson was the very experienced company check airman who helped mold me. As part of the IOE for Ryan Air, I had to learn the airplane, then the villages, and the routes to those villages along with the imposing terrain that I would have to negotiate at night in snow storms and limited visibility. It was a daunting task and had to be digested one small bite at a time. It was exactly the intense type of work that I wanted to do. I was embracing my fantasy with gusto.

During that orientation period in Kotzebue, I traveled with regular line pilots flying scheduled trips. It was a very busy time and occupied long hours most every day. Since Boris and I lived upstairs in the hangar, it wasn't hard to get to work early and stay late. There was an incident on one of those regularly scheduled flights to nearby Selawick where Dick Kock (pronounced Cook) was flying low-level in the dark.

Most of the terrain between Kotzebue and Selawik is flat (Selawik Lake) except one slight rise. While the wintertime darkness precluded almost any forward visibility, you could make out the terrain, looking straight down. Yes, that's right. You could see where you were, but not where you were going. To be prudent; first, you must know where you are and have a minimum safe enroute altitude (MEA) well established in your mind for the trip. Somehow that day Dick failed to hold his altitude enroute and drifted below the MEA. Suddenly, violently, and without warning the 207 that he was flying bolted skyward. The nose pitched up in a disorienting display of disobedience. After he had regained control and settled his passengers, he realized that he had just flown into the ground at a very shallow angle. Beads of sweat formed on my forehead just hearing the story. Wow, if it happened to an experienced line pilot; it could also happen to me. Following that incident, we referred to him as Ricochet Dick! I learned a valuable lesson from his little story.

After I had been cleared by the company to carry passengers, I made an interesting discovery on a return trip one day. About 90 miles north of Kotzebue, the Red Dog Mine was the largest open pit mine in Alaska that I would witness from the air. The world's biggest zinc mine opened for business in 1989. It lay in the DeLong Mountains of the remote western Brooks Range and was discovered by a bush pilot on the Native-owned land. Today, ore concentrate is trucked from the mine 55 miles west to dedicated but isolated docks on the Chukchi Sea. Although mining takes place 24/7, the zinc ore is stored on the coast in massive buildings and shipped to market only when the remote port is ice-free.

For easy reference, I constructed a small personal Ryan Air notebook from index cards that were cut in half and carefully sewn together with red dental floss using a locking stitch. The compact reference listed all the airports and villages that were my regular destinations. I drew a detailed runway diagram with my exact time and heading to and from Kotzebue and or any other linking villages. The information included field elevation and the minimum enroute altitude needed to fly between airfields with adequate ground clearance. I also made notations of the radio, both local traffic, and company frequencies, along with any navigational aids or non-directional beacons that might benefit me. This prized reference helped me keep villages straight in my head, like the difference between Shungnak and Shageluk. Shungnak is on the Kobuk River, while Shageluk is southeast of Grayling and has an abandoned C-119 along the east side of the north end of the runway. To this day, that cherished little notebook is a tangible reminder of those dark stormy missions and that rocky beginning. I found it curious that the majority of village graveyards seemed to be visible from the airport, most notably at the approach end of the runway. I'm not sure why. A constant reminder for pilots, it was a bit disconcerting at first, but I got used to it as being "normal."

ALAKANUK   AUK

θ 297°-117° 52 NM -.25.5 MIN.

7.6 NM 205° RADIAL 117.8 ENM

CTAF 122.9

JOHN 122.9   18

                    ELEV 10'

                    2100 GVL

          36

UNUSABLE WEST HALF IN SPRING

ANIAK ANI

θ UNK 328°-148° 141 NM.

θ 85°-265° (KSM) 108 NM

θ BET 215°-35° 81 NM

CTAF 122.1   359 ANI

L/V 122.1   88°

RCO 122.15   1.7 NM

APP 125.2   10

LOC/DME 109.7

          ELEV 88

          6000'

AWOS 124.3

                    28

The little notebook I put together in Kotzebue to keep me and my passengers safe. Photographer Randy Lippincott.

During orientation, the station manager gave me some practical advice. He said that I should always make sure the village elder sits in the copilot seat. I reassured him that of course, I would, out of respect. Dale's response was a quick NO, not out of respect; it was to use him as a navigation tool. The elder will set there stoically staring straight ahead until you notice him slowly turn his head looking out his side window. It is called the Eskimo ADF, and he will be looking at his village—the one that you just passed in the dark.

An exciting trip for a young low-time pilot came with my assignment of a charter to Cape Romanzof LRRS Airport, a military destination. Located on the west coast between Scammon Bay and Hooper Bay, the isolated airfield was constructed to service the Cape Romanzof Long Range Radar Station. My approach was over a considerable distance of open frigid ocean with extensive areas of pack ice alternating with the open waters of the Norton Sound. Of course, no life jacket or exposure suit was available to me in the single engine Cessna. If anything happened over the open water, it would be a one-way trip. Since I had no prior experience in the remote area, my best guess was to aim at a fixed point on the coastline, intentionally offset from my destination. Once I intercepted the shoreline, I had to turn right or southbound and follow the coast until I spotted the cryptic runway. In a short while, it suddenly appeared; I had guessed correctly. I was already at 500 feet, and able to quickly add landing flaps to make the 90 degree left hand turn onto final over the water and land. There was no possibility of a go-around because the mountain was in the way. The windsock at the end of the runway helped me adjust my airspeed, and it was apparent that the very wide gravel strip was up-sloping; almost, but not quite as much as a ski jump. The one-way runway was designed to land uphill, and the takeoff was in the opposite direction, downhill and over the dark ice-choked water.

I was met by the military police, delivered my cargo, and was taking off over the imposing ocean in windy conditions in only a few minutes. The reciprocal of my flight path was not as straight forward because I hadn't thought it through as well as I should have. I made my best heading estimate, and soon the now familiar shoreline of Norton Sound came into view.

Landing was a skill that required precision because runway length or orientation was not always ideal. My intention was that I needed to touch down at the end of the runway every time to be able to stop on the runway. Conventional methods of power management were modified. Once I had the aircraft configured for final approach, the rate of descent and the point of touchdown was adjusted only with the throttle. Pilots refer to it as "dragging it in." On occasion, the landing could only be facilitated in one direction, and takeoff had to be in the opposite, no matter which way the wind was blowing. Just as in the execution of the Cape Romanzof landing, controlling my airspeed and consistency of my approach was everything.

St. Mary's Boys

Eventually, I was stationed with Ryan Air in the small native village of St. Mary's on the lower Yukon River. There I was willingly initiated into the high risk, hard labor, and the mentally stressful world of an air taxi pilot. I flew in the harsh, unforgiving, coastal weather of the dark, windy, and bitter cold of the Alaskan "bush." A pass/fail exercise, I knew friends who did not make the grade and will never have another chance. I was forced to hone aviation and navigation skills quickly to survive; it increased my confidence, which bred risk taking. Every day I pushed the envelope to do "a routine job." I systematically compromised safety for the dollar. Everybody else was flying in marginal conditions; I matter-of-factly accepted the real-world consequences. Close calls earned names like "One-way Ray," and "Ricochet Dick." Rules on the Last Frontier were left open to interpretation, and not everyone came home at night. Alaska's air safety record was far from pristine.

I had a near miss one day in St. Mary's. I was departing to the north in a fully loaded 207. Usually, I exercised good radio discipline, but for some reason, either I missed the other pilot's call, or he blocked mine. Possibly one of us had the radio set up incorrectly. I just didn't pay attention to the departure end of the runway, as it had never been an issue before in broad daylight. Of course, it was too late after I rotated, became airborne, and the much larger Cessna Caravan appeared directly in front of me at about 200 feet. He made no attempt to deviate as if I weren't even there. I'm sure he never saw me. It was destined to be an ugly midair fireball. At the last possible second, I made an extreme evasive maneuver to my right. There was nothing else to do at that point; the near miss was already history. I never did figure out exactly what happened, but I do know that I didn't have any control over the other airplane. With my heart seeming to beat out of my chest and sweat evaporating on my brow, it was a real awakening for me. The typical mid-air collision statistically happens near the airport. Gee, I guess that's why they call them accidents.

On the lower Yukon River, I had days of routine scheduled flying and other days of special sanctioned flights. Some of my most memorable charters were corpses, canines, and TV crews. Now, no stiff ever caused me grief, but my first dogsled charter in a 207 nearly killed me. It took place in Alakanuk, Alaska, and the "Assassins" were all cleverly disguised. They looked just like an innocent team of Alaskan Huskies ready to pull a sled.

The aircraft was configured upon my arrival with a large blue tarp covering the entire cabin floor. First, I easily loaded the small sprint sled in the otherwise open fuselage of the long airplane. Once I had it secured, I fastened a single line from the front of the plane to the back of the cabin. Then I clipped in each dog, nicely separated, on this single line. The Huskies were not unruly, just somewhat frisky and a little skittish; and I assumed the dogs were going to stay in their assigned positions. I secured the back doors of the airplane and taxied out to the snow-packed runway for takeoff. Anyone who has flown as a pilot understands that the two most critical phases of flight are takeoff and landing because the aircraft is at its slowest airspeed and the margin of safety for stalling the wing and causing a crash is quite narrow. To stall the wing means that the air no longer goes over the top of it creating lift necessary for flight. If it is close to the ground, then there is no time to recover from the frequently fatal event. To recover from a stall at altitude is usually manageable.

As I accelerated down the runway, everything seemed "ops normal," other than a few departing howls from the reluctant passengers. However, at the most critical point in the flight, which is just after rotation and above ground effect, all of the dogs collectively ran to the back of the aircraft. The abrupt movement caused the nose to pitch up dramatically, and the aircraft should have stalled immediately. I had a flashback to Challis, Idaho, and the last critical spin that I suffered. At that point, the dogs became a giant lever arm and should have forced an instantaneous stall in the extra-long Cessna 207, resulting in a tragic crash and burn off the departure end of the runway. It would have been another Alaskan statistic, and the executioner's work would have been complete. Without realizing what had just happened, but with lightning reflexes, I forced the nose downward toward the ground to maintain my airspeed and the wing's proper angle of attack. My spontaneous and automatic response saved my canine passengers and me.

It was a struggle, but I was able to accelerate back in ground effect out of the critical situation and managed the remaining tenuous portion of the flight at a safe altitude without further surprises from the pelted mob. Once I leveled the aircraft, the dogs, seemingly accustomed to the drone of the engine settled down for the remainder of the trip. The shifting angle of the floor and high pitch of the engine, at takeoff power, had collectively spooked the dogs. Fortunately, there was no obstacle near the end of the runway, or it would have impaled me. I used extra caution and airspeed landing in Kotlik. I made only very slight pitch changes in the controls and primarily used the throttle to descend and make a docile landing. I did not let those sons-of-bitches derail my career, and I dodged another Arctic bullet!

An unbelievable but true detail about the lower Yukon Delta is related to the following: One of the routine destinations out of St. Mary's was Bethel, 100 miles to the southeast. It was a sizable remote village on the ancient, vast lower Yukon-Kuskokwim River floodplain. Other than scattered lakes and the Kuskokwim River, it was 100 percent tundra. There were absolutely no trees to be found well past the horizon in all directions. Any kid who had grown up there and never traveled very far from home could truthfully say that he had never seen a real tree in his entire life.

I am often asked if I carried passengers or just hauled freight; I would have to answer yes to both; on occasion, both at the same time. I also flew charters for special events, the Forest Service, and tourists. Alaska is an unusual state because they have a special arrangement with the United States Postal Service. The airlines make rural mail delivery possible, and the USPS subsidizes the flights to all of the remote villages under a program called "Bypass." In the "bush," whether you order Pampers, pop, or bricks, it comes in the mail. Because the USPS is not able to access the remote villages by road, they contract the airlines to deliver the goods. Since the individual orders are usually palletized, they come to the hanger where a postal worker weighs it as it is loaded on the plane, so it "Bypasses" the physical post office. Therefore, all mail flown to over 400 villages that are not connected by any roads is referred to as "Bypass." In 2014, the United States Postal Service paid $108 million to airlines in Alaska for a program that produced only \$32 million in postal revenues.[10] The same system has been in place for the last 43 years.

The Longest Day

St. Mary's was my first assignment after my IOE with Ryan Air in Kotzebue, Alaska. I lived in a dorm style apartment with three other young pilots who flew for Ryan Air. Whenever Dale Walters came to check on us, he traditionally prepared a special breakfast of Krusteaz pancakes for his "boys." In fact, we looked forward to his visits. St. Mary's was a small village, and we walked everywhere except to the airfield. For that, we had a company truck that we drove the seven miles to the airport. The north-south runway was situated on a hill northwest of the St. Mary's village; both were virtually on the mighty Yukon River. There was a small terminal building where we frequently had to shovel large snow drifts to access the front door in the early morning light.

My daily trek from the company apartment in St. Mary's to the snowbound airfield was frequently arduous. The airport, on a hill northwest of the village, was often stormed in for days at a time. Working or waiting for it to clear, there were no easy days for the air taxi pilot. From those countless hours spent at the St. Mary's Station, waiting for the coastal weather to improve, I had sufficient time to ponder my neophyte aviation status. Often the view from the top of the hill was obscured by blowing snow.

Although the airplanes were parked outside, the engines were heated and covered with an insulated quilt for warmth and to keep out the snow. The nacelle cover would accompany the aircraft during the day. If an anticipated stop was going to take longer than ten minutes, the engine was covered to retain heat in the remote, frigid environment. Each aircraft was plugged in at night to keep the oil liquid and the battery warm to maintain the cranking power. Due

---

10   http://www.linns.com/news/postal-news/262/Alaska-bypass-mail-program-creating-division-in-the-House

to the coastal proximity and Arctic conditions, aircraft icing was a constant worry. To mitigate any potential fuel line icing, we always added a generous amount of glycol to the aviation gas. The wintertime work day conditions ranged from -20° to -45° Fahrenheit. Any off-airport landing would result in a critical survival situation. These circumstances would become exponentially more complicated with passengers to protect. Therefore, the cutoff for all flights was -50° Fahrenheit. Not because it was that much harder on equipment, but because of the consequences of an emergency landing. In the colder temperatures ice fog tended to form, and due to obscured visibility, it was just as dangerous as any other fog.

While I was stationed in St. Mary's, Alaska, I experienced my first 13-hour day of actual flight time. I flew nearly 8 hours commercially and 5.6 hours privately. As a pilot for Ryan Air, I was tasked to fly the Cessna 207 under FAR part 135. The federal regulations were strictly upheld and to go over the maximum eight-hour flight time limit was to suffer a penalty and suspension of your license. My routing that day called for the total of nearly eight hours flight time. It was defined as the time when the tires started moving for takeoff until they stopped rolling upon landing and was all carefully logged for my wages. I made the rounds to three villages during my long work day: Sheldon's Point, Mountain Village, and Emmonak. I was not paid for time at work that I was not flying the airplane. Typically, I would spend around 14 hours a day in the work environment.

Flying is a hard way to earn an easy living.[11]

It was the first day of spring and a Friday. Fortunately, I was due to rotate back to Fairbanks for a well-deserved rest at the end of my extremely long day. After turning in my logs and securing the company 207, I performed the preflight on my personal Cessna 172 in the dim light. When satisfied with the condition of the Skyhawk, I took off on the six-hour trip to Fairbanks and a well-deserved rest with my family; I was now under FAR Part 91 rules (non-commercial). I

---

[11]   http://funnyairlinestories.com/pilot_stuff/pilot_sayings.asp

had a comfortable fuel reserve after an intermediate stop in McGrath. It was 5.6 hours on top of the 7.3 hours of commercial flying, for a total of 12.9 hours that day. I had not been in the air long when complete darkness fell over me. Because the light had faded gradually, my eyes easily adjusted to the single little cabin red light and the brilliant outside palpable starlight that drew me forward. Soon, I realized to my amazement that the glow in the windscreen was coming from the very fluid Aurora Borealis. Now, this was a double-edged sword—the optics of the night sky versus the true horizon was obscured. The Aurora was beautiful and captivating and the night sky was mesmerizing and crystal clear. The stars were dazzling, and I felt like I was flying under a giant arch of the very visible Milky Way. I could see the occasional silent shooting star as if to compete for my attention, saying, "Hey look over here."

My eyes were continuously teased outside toward the spectacular view, but I needed to pay close attention to the instruments in the plane and my position over the ground. The artificial horizon formed by the Northern Lights was subtle and deceptive. When I did look outside and focus on the Aurora, I forced myself to relax my hands on the steering column so that I would not start an improper and insidious turn while trying to match the false and alluring horizon. This distraction was very unexpected and a new phenomenon for me on this long tiring trip. Because I had to hand fly the 172 (no autopilot), my attention needed to be focused on the critical instrument panel and not on the deceptive illusion in the visible outside environment. Typically, while flying in the clouds, only the instrument panel gives the pilot in command guidance for straight and level, that is, safe flight. Now, looking outside at the Aurora gave maximal and convincing disinformation. Not only was it moving, but in very indistinct ways generated the impression that I was already in a turn. If I were to succumb to this input, that is, fly by the "seat of my pants," the aircraft would soon be spinning out of control in the night sky somewhere in the frozen wilderness! The tendency toward spatial disorientation reared its ugly head.

I knew that it was more important than ever that I concentrate on the task at hand. I felt the fatigue of a long workday, the oppressive veil of night, and the irrepressible optical illusion of the normally friendly Northern Lights. All of that along with an outside temperature of -40° Fahrenheit. My cross-country navigating was primarily by dead reckoning along the north edge of the massive, towering, and dangerous Alaska Range.

> There are certain aircraft sounds that
> can only be heard at night.[12]

I played mind games and sang to myself to keep my brain active and to stay awake. I was continuously flying the airplane, checking and rechecking my position on the map for safety's sake. I began to think about Lindbergh enduring more than 33 hours of sleep deprivation as he crossed the Atlantic and the assistance from his "angels." It was at the ten-hour interval into Lindbergh's flight that he first noted: "strange passengers" that would help him complete his epic trip. Would I need support from my personal angel to complete my journey? Long before it was within range, I dialed in the Fairbanks control tower frequency. Nearly 30 minutes from landing, I was able to contact air traffic control. There was no activity to occupy the tower operator, and at that point, I asked him for a favor. He willingly called my wife to let her know when I was landing and to please pick me up. As the welcome lights of Fairbanks came into view, I started to breathe easier on the final leg of my long and circuitous journey that day. It had been a punishing but rewarding very long "13 hour day," and I was happy to be home.

Flying the "Hudson River Valley"

In the spring, I was transferred to Aniak with Ryan Air. This scenic, isolated small village was on the Kuskokwim River south of a major bend in the Yukon River. The canyon upriver from Aniak reminded me of a wild and scenic Hudson River Valley on the East

---

[12] http://funnyairlinestories.com/pilot_stuff/pilot_sayings.asp

Coast. It was beautiful, and the people were friendly. While living there, I rented a large unfinished basement from an agreeable local family with several young children. Linda was my station manager, and her daughter's name was Rhiannon. Yes, named after the 1975 Fleetwood Mac song of the same name. If I wasn't headed up the remote and scenic Kuskokwim River, I was flying north and into villages on the lower Yukon River. It was to be my last assignment with Ryan Air, and I would come to miss it. Late that spring I got word that Larry's Flying Service was hiring. I took the job and moved back to Fairbanks and into my house, but I was never completely forgiven by my family for being gone. You see, while I was away, our cat Tiger died.

The experience I gained at Ryan Air under the tutelage of Dale Walters was invaluable to me. In six months, I gained a lifetime of experience...and more gray hair. The natives told me that they trusted a pilot with gray hair status, so I had the color thing going for me. Walters was one hell of a station manager, and I would have followed him anywhere. Years later, Dale moved to Fairbanks and was involved in a near-fatal car accident when he was T-boned on the driver's side. He suffered a debilitating head injury and tragically was never able to fly again. It made me sick that Dale could survive World War II, crop dusting, working as a primary flight instructor, multiple transpacific single engine ferry flights, a lifetime of hazardous flying, but suffer a serious injury driving in the city. Ultimately he succumbed at age 90 following complications from a hip fracture.

I had planned all along to apply for a job in Fairbanks and move back in with my family. As it turned out, the pilot standing in the door is the guy who gets the job offer; and that's the way it went with Larry's Flying Service. They had summer positions open, and I was available to start work anytime they had an opening for me. Summer was busy with routine schedules, flying for the Fire Service and tourist charters. My flights would be in a single engine airplane that first season until I had a minimum of 1,500 total hours and my twin rating. Those were the minimal requirements for the twin-engine Airline Transport Pilot's license. At that point, I could fly passengers in almost all weather conditions and log much more regular time on the longer routes.

Larry's Flying Service

John's death was unnecessary. John R. Hitz joined Larry's Flying Service during the winter of 1992-3. Not only was he likable, but he was a fellow Nebraskan, which was icing on the cake for me. John took up residence in a local log cabin with no running water. He had electricity but cut and burned firewood to heat his humble chalet. I believe it was for the "Alaskan experience" and partly because John was on a budget. He was a young and carefree soul who loved life and had a passion for flying. I was excited to watch him grow and share in his Alaskan adventures. He procured a snowmachine as a typical means of winter transportation. It is an excellent way to get around in the winter. You can virtually go anywhere. The rivers are frozen, the roads are snow packed, and in the wilderness, there are no barbed wire fences to spoil your day.

The 28-year-old John was out on Friday, January 8, 1993. He was playing in the dark, making new tracks in the deep snow with his snowmachine like a young man might cut loose after work on a Friday. In the excitement of a small challenge of a steep embankment, John suddenly turned to mount a large snow berm and instantly burst onto a plowed road. As it turned out, the highway was part of a busy overpass, and traffic was rapidly approaching in the far lane. At the last possible instant, the truck may have registered out of John's peripheral vision, but there was no time to stop. The momentum that had taken him up the embankment carried him across the street and into the path of the oncoming vehicle. In a flash, his life was taken from him. Everyone grieved John's passing. It was a sad day when I met his parents when they came to take their boy home. The irony of the event was that except for the snow, his situation was almost identical to my motorcycle accident when I was 15. Only somehow I was spared, and his life was forfeited. It didn't seem fair.

High Flight

...I have slipped the surly bonds of earth,
Put out my hand, and touched the face of God.
— John Gillespie Magee Jr.
19-year-old American killed in action,
World War II

In preparation for the ATP license I had to pass a written exam, have earned a commercial pilot's license, an instrument rating, and have a current Class I physical. I never imagined that the physical exam was going to be an issue when I picked the Airman's Medical Examiner (AME) from the Tanana Valley Clinic. In fact, I failed the flight physical due to the Ishihara color blindness test. About 8 percent of men and 0.5 percent of women are affected by a similar color vision deficiency. Born "color blind," I was more than just a little irritated. I had been flying for well over 20 years and had never failed a physical. Yes, I had issues with the Ishihara plates but was always given some leeway on the exam. Unfortunately, when it counted toward my livelihood, I was failed by an examiner who lacked empathy.

My appeal to the FAA was in the form of a practical exam. The first part was daytime and the second part was at night. The FAA examiner sat with me in the front seat of his car as we drove to the far end of the runway during the daylight portion. At that point, the tower gave me a series of light signals. I was able to identify each without difficulty. The second part of the exam that winter was in my 172 in complete darkness. The examiner in the right front seat asked me to identify the colors of different lights even as we taxied out to the end of 19 right in Fairbanks. After takeoff, we climbed to pattern altitude in the darkness. I had to identify colored lights while flying around the city. Once I jumped through all of those hoops, I was issued a permanent colorblindness waiver. In other words, I had a red-green deficiency, but it did not compromise my flight safety.

The medical profession is the natural enemy
of the aviation profession.[13]

The ATP

To qualify for the Airline Transport Pilot License requires a total of at least 1,500 hours of pilot-in-command (PIC) time. The instrument, commercial, and twin-engine ratings are required as prerequisites to the twin-engine ATP License. The inspector is also supposed to determine whether the candidate is of "Good Moral Character," to qualify. I don't recall if anyone asked me about my moral references or if they could just tell by looking at me. With this license, I would be able to work in marginal weather conditions and carry passengers anywhere my company flew. This certificate gave me the opportunity to fly more regular hours along with an increase in pay.

I reached my 1,500-hour goal while working at Larry's Flying Service that summer and was anxious to get my twin-engine rating. We traveled to Nebraska for the holidays, and during that winter visit, I spent an intense three days in Omaha getting checked out in a twin Beechcraft Duchess. Following that, I took my multiengine, instrument checkride to ATP standards. I did most of my flying at night, which substantially helped my confidence during the checkride.

The workload difference between a single and twin-engine aircraft is exponentially increased when done to ATP standards and in an artificially compressed period. Most of the single-engine planes that I had been flying were fixed gear. The Duchess not only had twice as many levers to operate and gauges to monitor but also had retractable gear to incorporate into the mandatory checklist. I simply didn't have enough experience in the twin to develop any concrete routine or "muscle memory" along with a certain degree of confidence.

I had over 1,000 hours VFR flight in the past year, but it was all in single-engine, fixed gear aircraft. It was going to be tough to

---

[13] http://funnyairlinestories.com/pilot_stuff/pilot_sayings.asp

break those lifetime habits and casual VFR mindset. To qualify for the ATP, I had to be able to operate the twin in the IFR environment (no available outside visual reference) and perform all types of instrument approaches with precision. My transition was not as straightforward as it might seem, but I had essentially been doing the same thing at night in the Alaskan dark and snowy conditions in single engine aircraft.

Now I needed to be comfortable in the twin-engine airplane, know all of its systems, and become proficient in emergency procedures (read that single-engine drills). The most critical exercise with a twin-engine aircraft is the pilot's first response to an engine failure on takeoff. The foolproof method was, "dead foot (you no longer needed to press on that rudder pedal), dead engine!" The exercise helped the pilot avoid feathering the propeller and shutting down the WRONG engine close to the ground, therefore ensuring a crash. The procedure of feathering or turning the propeller blades into the wind decreased the drag on the failed engine and increased the chances of survival. Vmc (velocity-minimum controllable) was the slowest controllable airspeed if the critical engine stopped working. If the pilot was below this airspeed during an engine failure, the operative engine had enough torque to roll the aircraft over on its back close to the ground—a fatal mistake!

Shooting instrument approaches in the twin-engine aircraft on ONE ENGINE was something I had to practice to be proficient. Those approaches had to be precise and within the ATP standards. Simultaneously, I had to be able to assimilate all of those critical skills, adequately perform them, and stay ahead of the slippery little airplane. It all added up to a very high level of stress!

Finally, over the three-day period, I had flown enough time in the Beechcraft Duchess to take my twin-engine/ATP checkride. Looking back, I am amazed that it was possible to accomplish that in a short 72-hour period. I was scheduled that third night for the check flight at Eppley Field in Omaha. We took off for the masochistic exercise after the examiner was satisfied with my knowledge of the airplane. At first, the flight was night VFR. For me, the Duchess was a very fast plane and, initially, it was hard to stay ahead of it mentally. In other words,

I gained altitude rapidly, reached my waypoints quicker, and had to think faster to stay in control. The accelerated sequence was not a natural pace for me to sustain. I had to anticipate well ahead of what I was accustomed. Any mistakes would snowball and quickly spin out of control. When the examiner was satisfied with my initial performance, he had me don the hood. The hood is a visibility restrictive device so that the pilot being tested has absolutely no outside visual reference even though it's at night.

I entered the hold at the designated fix as I reached the assigned altitude. After a couple of turns, I was instructed to "shoot the ILS" approach. I descended to the assigned altitude, adjusted the airspeed, and intercepted the localizer inbound. I re-established the power setting and was waiting to intercept the glideslope when Loren started kicking me under the seat. Oh yeah, I forgot to tell you my little Air Force F-16 brother was riding along on the checkride for harassment purposes. Apparently, he was worried that I had forgotten to lower my landing gear. The correct procedure was to lower the landing gear upon glideslope intercept. The extra drag allowed the aircraft to slow down and descend at the same time. I guess he couldn't see the glideslope needles from the backseat.

I knew what I had to do, but it was almost like the first time you try to rub your belly and pat your head in front of an audience. I felt like my head was going to explode, and I experienced momentary "mind lock." I can truthfully say it was mentally the most taxing experience I ever had to overcome under a severe time constraint. I was flying new equipment, a complex twin-engine (for the first time), at night with the hood on for a realistic IFR environment, down to very tight ATP standards—along with emergency procedures thrown in. All of my prior experience had been flying in a relaxed VFR (visual flight rules, you can look outside and see the horizon) non-precision environment. I desperately wanted the APT, having traveled all the way from Fairbanks, Alaska. The self-induced pressure did not help.

Yes, the checkride was extremely demanding; in fact, it was exhausting, but in the end, I was very proud of my success. I was gratified to have the new unrestricted ATP ticket in my pocket.

At that moment, all of my intense efforts and drama seemed a bit anti-climactic. The new license meant that I would be eligible to be checked out in the Piper Navajo Chieftain in Fairbanks. Larry's Flying Service had six Chieftains; so other than the -50° Fahrenheit restriction, I would be flying continuously throughout the winter. And that's pretty much how it went that first season, six days a week. My work days were fourteen hours long. Typically, I was paid for six or seven hours, the total time that I was in the air, or the total time from when the wheels started rolling to when they stopped back on the ground.

Fifty Below Zero and Ice Fog

I did fly a fair amount the first winter in single engine aircraft. But by the second winter, I had learned everything about the Chieftain and how to handle it. I loved that airplane! When I closed the crew-door behind me every morning, I felt like I was putting on a pair of my favorite comfortable old broken-in blue jeans. During the time I flew the Piper Navajo Chieftain, our official company cut off was -50° Fahrenheit or dense ice fog. The temperature limit was not for the pilot or the equipment, but rather the passengers. If we had a mechanical problem in a remote location, there was no way to ensure the safety and survivability of the passengers at that temperature. Although it was an arbitrary figure, I could tell that all things mechanical started to protest when it was greater than 45 below zero. Yes, there were close calls, hardships, and long hours of toil. But I got to sit in the front seat for the greatest wilderness show on Earth. I've flown everywhere north of the Alaskan range and landed on each and every runway along the expanse of the Alaskan Yukon River. It was the best time of my life! I only wish it had lasted longer.

Randy Lippincott in front of one of Larry's Flying Service
Piper Navajo Chieftains. Photographer unknown.

Now and then, I had a little fun at work. One morning I took off
with a mechanic on a ferry flight to Galena in a Navajo. As soon as
we were out of the traffic pattern, Bob pulled out the daily newspaper.
I knew that he was nicely distracted and instead of leveling off at
12,000 feet in the empty Chieftain, I climbed right up to 24,000 feet
westbound. I had summited McKinley at 20,320 feet and knew that
I could easily tolerate the thin air for a short period. Now, maybe the
altitude reporting portion of the transponder was inoperative at this
point because you're not supposed to ascend above 18,000 feet without
an explicit clearance from ATC. Above 18,000 feet is considered
Positive Controlled Airspace.

After the extended climb, I turned to Bob and asked him if
he wanted to fly the airplane. He was tickled by the offer and
immediately took over the control wheel. In a couple of minutes,
I suggested that we start our descent into Galena. Bob dutifully
complied but was a bit puzzled after the altimeter unwound 12,000
feet and we were still sitting at 12,000 feet. "Now how could that be?"
Bob stated rhetorically. I just looked at the mechanic and told him that

he had to continue his descent 12,000 feet if we were going to make it down in time to land in Galena. Just like that, Bob responded, "Well that would mean we were at 24,000 feet." No shit, Sherlock! Bob remarked that he thought he had been a little short of breath while reading the obituaries, and now he knew why. Luckily he wasn't going to have to give up smoking after all.

In my travels, I had the opportunity to fly over the largest caribou herd I had ever witnessed for several days in a row. Village elders told me that there was an area of 5,000 caribous north of Galena in the Koyukuk National Wildlife Refuge. When I first spotted them, it was with a quiet gasp of astonishment as I realized that I had discovered the massive gathering of spectacular wildlife. The landscape suddenly appeared to be alive. I wished that I could have landed to spend more time observing the beautiful herd of native animals. The temptation to buzz them in a responsible fashion was irresistible. The realization that few people in the world would ever get to see something like this up close in the wild made me feel special and want more. It was my private, self-directed safari with a National Geographic backdrop— and someone else was paying for the fuel.

I experienced that same feeling of awe when I flew over a full-sized Kodiak grizzly. I spotted the massive bear from afar on the open tundra and circled back to have a better look. I slowed down and went down to observe the bear in its habitat. The grizzly, no kidding, wanted to fight. My very presence had violated his personal space. As I flew over, he was standing on his enormous hind legs and was desperately pawing the air. In no uncertain terms, he wanted to take on the giant flying machine. That carnivore was trying to pull the large airplane out of the sky with his lethal claws. The magnificent bear was at the top of the food chain, had no natural enemies, and therefore, knew no fear. To come upon the imposing predator suddenly and up close was a burst of pure adrenaline. I was glad that I was not meeting him on a level playing field.

There Was an Emergency

I had very few valid complaints with the maintenance department at Larry's, but a propeller governor cable was one of them. It was midsummer, unusually hot, and I was at or over my weight limit in the Chieftain. I had nine large passengers and a lot of baggage and knew that everything had to go perfectly for a safe trip. I used the full length of the runway at Kobuk and departed to the west over the Kobuk River. A minute after rotation I retarded the RPM for the climb out. Immediately, I recognized that the left engine was not responding to my control input, and I knew that I had a runaway engine. Due to the heavy load, I wanted to continue my climb out as I turned to the south until I had the landing in nearby Galena assured. I did not consider it prudent to try and return to the small and short gravel runway at Kobuck.

That's the thing about emergencies—you never know when you are going to have one!

However, first, I had to make a decision on whether to shut down an engine that I could not feather (turning the propeller blade into the wind to cause as little drag as possible) or risk destroying the motor and possibly resulting in a fire. I immediately contacted the Galena tower and declared an emergency. The engine overspeed started to heat up and was approaching a catastrophic failure. At that point, I knew that I was near enough to the Galena runway, had enough altitude, and I felt it prudent to shut down the defective engine. Still unable to feather the prop, I knew that it would cause significant asymmetric drag and cause the airplane to yaw. My focus was on the operative engine. While in the cruise power setting, I was unable to maintain altitude with the extremely heavy airplane. I started my calculated and involuntary descent onto the emergency equipped airfield, aware that I had some reserve power in the right engine if absolutely necessary. Usually, at the time of an accident, it is more than a single issue. My problems were several: over max gross weight, decreased lift due to the hot day, increased drag on the left engine (first a runaway engine and now my inability to feather the propeller), my first experience with a runaway engine, and now excessive strain on the operative motor.

Slightly closer to Galena I initiated my best approach. My plan was to intercept the extended runway centerline and precisely configure the aircraft for a straight-in landing. I had to remain above the normal glideslope to give myself an extra margin of error. Now, things were happening rapidly. I gradually reduced the power on the right engine slightly, which relieved the yaw factor (pulling to the left); and only when I felt the landing was assured did I commit and lower the flaps and gear a few seconds before touching down. This drag slowed the aircraft dramatically for a conventional landing. A rush of relief swept through me as I taxied clear of the runway. Right turns were impossible with the dead left engine, and I used my momentum and differential breaking to carry me onto the tarmac and away from the fire-engines. The concerned passengers quietly deplaned. No one said "Good job or thanks." They just wanted their baggage.

When the company mechanic arrived, the troubleshooting took only two minutes. A loose bracket on the engine had caused the propeller governor cable to malfunction. The unfortunate episode could have ended much differently on that sweltering day. I didn't know enough to report it to the Feds, but I did know that my job could be in jeopardy if I had complained about it to Larry.

During my parent's annual visit, the only flight my mother scheduled to accompany me in the Chieftain was to fly across the Arctic Circle. We departed Fairbanks to the north on the way to Fort Yukon and the notable crossing of the Arctic Circle. However, minutes into the climb-out I saw black smoke coming out of the left engine and experienced a slight loss of power. The left turbocharger had failed. While I started to turn back to the airfield, I notified the tower that we were returning to land. That was the first and last turbocharger to ever fail on me. Mom never did make it across the Arctic Circle on the way to Fort Yukon.

During all of my flight time in over a half century of flying, my only near fuel exhaustion moment was on a 382 nautical mile trip coming back from Kotzebue to Fairbanks. I had a last minute enroute diversion that should have required an opportunity to take on additional fuel; however, it did not. As far as gas went, I almost ALWAYS cheated. I habitually had more fuel than the trip required and sometimes more than the maximum weight allowed. This deviation was the only exception. I could have added extra 100LL if I had been given the trip from the beginning, but that was not the case; my schedule changed while I was in the air. My anxiety increased because I did not have favorable winds, and I fully expected that at least one of my engines would sputter to a stop before landing. In retrospect, I should have refused the rerouting. To minimize the problem, I climbed to a higher than usual altitude for the trip (better glide range and economy but stronger headwinds), I powered back both engines and leaned the mixture to the extreme maximum to save on precious petrol. I prayed and sweated little bullets until I started my last minute VFR descent into Fairbanks for the closest possible runway (direct to the numbers, at the end of the runway). I did not ask for priority handling, but would NOT have accepted any delay thrown at me. Somehow, the engines did not quit on the long taxi into the ramp across the airfield. Before I put the airplane away that night, I personally filled both tanks. My left tank had three gallons of fuel remaining, and my right tank had two gallons of avgas in it. Regrettably, I would have been the first one to the site of the accident. I never made that foolish mistake again after that singularly valuable and stressful lesson.

Pilots agree about the three basic things you cannot use when flying: 1) The runway behind you, 2) the altitude above you, and 3) the fuel in an empty tank.

170 Flight Hours in July

During my second summer with Larry's Flying Service, we planned a family sailing trip in Prince William Sound. My high school classmate Alan Glantz had offered to take my entire family out on Barnaby—his beautiful 46 foot Cruising Cal yacht. I was looking forward to the grand voyage. During the past year, I had worked feverishly, put in countless long hours, and even worked holidays. I did not think it unreasonable for me to take a week off in August to be with my family. Fortunately, I had requested the time well enough in advance to strike a deal with Larry. During July, I would have to work 31 straight days to make up the time in advance. I flew a total of 170 hours that month to "pay" for my vacation time. And, yes, the trip was well worth all of my efforts. Prince William Sound was a wonderfully placid and scenic waterway during our visit. Eight of my extended family members enjoyed six days on the yacht touring the magnificent Prince William Sound between Whittier and Valdez. We saw glaciers, dodged icebergs, heard whales, saw the northern lights, cascading waterfalls, native animals, and toured the wild and scenic archipelago in perfect weather. It was a stark contrast to the kayaking trip I had done in the same area three years prior.

Not only had I labored long hours each day in preparation for the outing, but also I had spent long hours in the pilot's chair. The seats in the Chieftain were mostly okay, but I developed an unusual problem. I experienced numbness and tingling on both sides of my posterior ribcage. It was minimally distracting, a bit disconcerting, and would completely resolve when not flying the very long hours. I can only guess that I was subject to a skin/nerve irritation from the long hours of high-frequency vibration to my torso in the mid-sized twin-engine airplane. I never did hear anyone else describe the same issue.

In the Alaska bush, I'd rather have a two-hour bladder and three hours of gas than vice versa.[14]

On a routine flight, I was at my normal cruising altitude in fair weather as I approached Nenana on the way back to Fairbanks. Far overhead, a fresh contrail ran from north to south. The sun's position and the humidity were just right because the contrail cast a visible linear shadow all the way to the ground, an incredible "gray curtain" of focused light and dark contrast. I have never seen this as perfectly dramatic before or since. In a short period, I physically passed through the palpable murkiness. As I looked down at the aircraft's shadow, I could see its visual halo, a "glory" far below me, as it passed in and out of the eerie light void. Wow, what a vivid and memorable visual distraction!

---

[14]   http://funnyairlinestories.com/pilot_stuff/pilot_sayings.asp

Delta Apology

I composed the following letter as a result of my parents' first "free flight" in 1990 on Delta Air Lines, compliments of their son, Delta pilot Loren Lippincott. As the letter explained, Dick and Rosalie had a chilling departure from Fairbanks International. My father was wearing a turtle neck under a polyester jacket when he checked in. At that time the ticket agent asked him to wear a tie, and Dad put one on—over his turtleneck. We joked about it in the terminal, and he played with it, twisting it first one way then the other. The midnight flight departed on time, and we were grateful for the off-season reunion.

December 3, 1990

Mr. H. R. Lippincott, Jr.
RXR1 2 Box 203
Central City, NE 68826

Dear Mr. Lippincott:

Sir, it has been brought to the attention of this department that you failed to maintain the dress standards required of any Delta employee or family members traveling non-revenue space available (NRSA).

Mr. Lippincott in order to provide an atmosphere of professional decor we have established these standards so as to best serve our paying passengers. We always ask our NRSA passengers to blend in, not bring attention to themselves and adhere to our dress code. Our gate agents have the responsibility to closely monitor these standards. Enclosed I send you a copy of the dress code. Again, sir we require a coat, and tie with a button down dress shirt.

Until you can agree to comply to these guidelines your pass privileges are hereby revoked. A copy of this letter will be placed in your son's file.

Sincerely,

DELTA PASS BUREAU

Carol E. Jones

Carol E. Jones
Supervisor

CEF/hrr

Later we called to thank Loren for the opportunity of the visit. I mentioned how Dad had been the comic relief with his tie. Perturbed by the deviation in protocol, my brother laid out a strategy to teach Father a lesson. The next day Loren composed a scathing letter on what appeared to be Delta stationery and mailed the unsanctioned note. Loren kept me apprised of the situation. On the phone, he read the citation that indefinitely revoked their flying pass privileges due to the violation.

Mother's call came Wednesday evening. "Randy, we're in serious trouble," she exclaimed. I switched the tape recorder on for posterity, and the fun began. Frantically, she rationalized their actions and pleaded for me to write a letter of apology for them. I seriously refused for a while, but she insisted that I design a letterhead and use my laser printer and "make it look official." Finally, I acquiesced and said that I'd draft the apology. Previously, I had saved the moronic apology made by the barrister in the movie *A Fish Called Wanda*. He was hung by his heels out of a second story window and forced to apologize for the error of his ways. I planned to make the letter a blend of just enough fact and movie to be ridiculous. When Mom and Dad received their copy to sign and forward to the Pass Bureau, they called Loren. He assured them that it required convincing language and was on target. Mother also called me and questioned whether the word malice was absolutely necessary. I did my best to lead them down the Primrose Path.

Loren instructed dad to send the signed letter to him and he would hand-carry it to the Pass Bureau. Nearly four agonizing weeks had passed before Loren admitted to the hoax. Dad was really pissed, but Mom was relieved that all her worrying had paid off. The folks promised that this was not to be the last Machiavellian apology.

H.R. Lippincott Jr. & Sons
Agriculture Specialists Since 1922

REGISTERED MAIL

Box 203, Route 2   December 7, 1990
Central City, Nebraska 68826

Dear Ms. Jones:

In reference to your letter dated December 3, 1990, regarding the Delta dress code, I wish to express my most sincere apology. This was our first NRSA (non revenue space available) trip!

It was not my intent to violate the Delta dress code. I felt properly dressed in the warmest clothes available to me. The midnight Fairbanks departure temperature was -35 degrees F. I was asked by your ticket agent in Fairbanks to put on a tie which I did promptly. I wore the tie and jacket until arriving home in Nebraska. My wife and I were placed in the front row in first class and were exposed to cold air for approximately one hour while on the ground in Anchorage. Much of the time was spent with the door open.

I feel that since this oversight has been brought to my attention I will unilaterally rectify it without delay. I plan to shop in earnest over the Holidays for a wardrobe suitable for Delta standards. I will be ready physically and mentally for my next NRSA trip.

Ms. Jones, I wish to apologize, I am really, really sorry. I apologize unreservedly. I would undo, if it were in my power. I hope to offer a complete and utter retraction of the event if I may. The imputation was totally without basis in fact and was in no way fair comment to the Delta image, and was motivated purely by malice. I deeply regret any distress my comments or actions may have caused you, or your company. I hereby undertake not to repeat any such breech of dress code at any time in the future.

Hopefully this apology meets Delta's requirements, and as a first offense the incident will not be reflected in my son's record. He is also a F-16 Fighting Falcon pilot.

Sincerely,

H.R. Lippincott Jr.
H.R. Lippincott Jr.

The response, on The Day that will Live in Infamy....

Earth, Wind, and Fire

Earth—It Will Smite You

It's called CFIT, and the accident reports are filled with them. Both Canadian low time pilot, David Evans and experienced Roger Gordon, my former chief pilot suffered the same fate. Roger was carrying a group of elders into the village of White Mountain on August 28, 1995. It was a short flight from Nome along the coast of Norton Sound. He was not on an IFR flight plan, and he was flying low-level with zero forward visibility in the clouds. I had traveled with Roger plenty of times when he exhibited this same behavior (confident of navigating in a cloud when he did not have objective confirmation of his exact location). This time he was using both his forward-looking radar in conjunction with a radar altimeter for terrain separation as he flew eastbound along the Norton Sound coast. At first glance, it all seemed reassuring.

He was not at the MEA (Minimum Enroute Altitude) for that trip segment. An MEA would have guaranteed terrain separation five miles either side of his planned route. He was unaware that he was not traveling across the ground in the same direction that his radar was "looking." Rather, he was flying with a strong crosswind from over the water, which made the airplane crab or "skid sideways" through the air. It was just enough to give him the false impression that he was avoiding high terrain along the coast; however, because the radar was "looking" out over the water, he was unaware of the mountain directly ahead of him. The radar altimeter would have indicated a safe altitude right up to the instant before impact. Roger would have been traveling nearly 200 mph, the normal cruise speed for this aircraft.

The pathophysiology of the crash indicated that they were, in fact, traveling in excess of 100 mph. At the time of impact, it generated considerably more than 60 Gs (one G is equal to your body weight, so the instantaneous force of 60 times your weight). There was a notation of a ruptured aorta, determined at autopsy. The sheer momentum and weight of the blood within the artery causes the large vessel to explode, unable to contain the overwhelming forces. It was over in a split second. The crash instantly killed everyone on board. This type of fatal error is often repeated in the Arctic and is an unfortunately calculated risk that frontier pilots frequently take.

Much of my commercial flying in Alaska also was low-level, with poor visibility, in high-risk aviation ventures, and with a mission to accomplish that was just like Roger's. Incredibly, it only takes one inappropriate action to end a life in this unforgiving environment. The tragedy occurred well after I had left Alaska, but it still made me feel sick inside since I knew the victims. I was sad for the families left behind to mourn the loss of loved ones. In fact, it could have been me. I had learned to push the envelope, not actually to cut corners, but I took calculated risks to do the challenging work. The pressure was mostly real, but it was a fact that if you couldn't accomplish the job, there was someone in line behind you waiting to take your place; that somehow justified pushing the envelope.

Wind—Cleared to Land on Any Surface

The Alaskan interior was usually calm, but the wind in Fairbanks that day, was the exception. May 27, 1989, I took Jim and Seamus Siddall, along with my wife Cathy, to Paxson on the Richardson Highway. We walked to the roadhouse for lunch and in a few hours were ready to return home. Going and coming through Isabel Pass (the Alaskan Range), we had good weather without any fanfare, turbulence, or cause for alarm. As we blissfully headed back to Fairbanks on the north side of the Alaska Range, it seemed like we were making excellent time in the smooth air.

As we got closer to town, I couldn't believe the Air Traffic Information Service (ATIS) when they announced that the winds were gusting to 50 knots! In everyday language, that means it was blasting over 57 mph; these were authentically severe gale force winds. I knew it wasn't because the jet stream had dipped down, even though that does happen over Alaska. That day the wind was blowing from the east—the wrong direction for the jet-stream. When I called the control tower, there was no negotiation; he just cleared me to land on ANY SURFACE. And, oh, by the way, good luck with that! I had never even heard or read of anything like that. Of course, in retrospect, I had plenty of fuel and should have diverted to nearby Fort Wainwright where the runways were correctly oriented. There was no other traffic to contend with at any local airport.

I carefully considered my options and made the decision to attempt the landing in the little Skyhawk with my three captive passengers. There was no doubt at that point; I knew what to do and lined up on the big east/west taxiway between 19R and 19L. I gently touched down directly into the gale-like headwind at a near hover. On the ground, I made the dangerous taxi with minimal turning; I headed straight for my tie-down spot on the far ramp. With the judicious use of the aileron, elevator, and rudder, I kept the wind from getting "under the wing." If it did, if it started to raise the wingtip, it would quickly flip the small bird over on its back with us in it. Slowly and cautiously, I taxied into a strategically tenable position. While still facing into the vicious wind, I had Jim exit and securely anchor the windward (the right wing nearest the wind source) wing. Then I shut down the airplane, and with help from all hands on board, we physically forced the aircraft out of its weathervane position and quickly chained the tail. Lastly, I secured the leeward (downwind) wing. It was satisfying to safely solve this artificial problem in the ridiculously windy conditions where it was a challenge to breathe and stand erect.

I must say that I had my share of poor to lousy weather, but most of the time the weather for the interior of Alaska was fair.

After spending a long day in a single engine airplane, I was returning to Fairbanks at night from "downriver" (Yukon River). The Fairbanks International Airport is oriented in a north-south configuration, and it is on the lee side of Chena Ridge. During the flight in question, the wind was particularly strong out of the west and generated unusually severe turbulence on the approach to landing at the airport. I cautiously set up the ILS for the 01L procedure in the pitch dark and centered the needles once on the localizer. I had no idea what lay ahead.

As I intercepted the extended centerline, I realized that I was in for a bumpy ride. The final segment turned out to be so turbulent that I was physically unable to focus on the instrument panel (the glideslope needles). I could occasionally see the runway lights dancing out ahead of me, could tell that I was still "right side up," and knew that I had started the approach at the appropriate altitude. I had to trust that the airplane was getting closer to the end of the runway. I could not focus on my panel. The jarring was so rapid and physically abusive that I was unable to clearly see the instruments. I worried about the enamel on my molars, as well as the wings on the plane. It was like an overly dramatic scene out of the movies. Fortunately, it smoothed out close to the ground, and my landing turned out to be a nonevent. I let out a sigh, realizing that I should never have to repeat that. The next morning I reported the violent turbulence to the mechanics to have the airplane checked out for serious cracks. Metal fatigue is not the pilot's friend.

Fairbanks International Airport looking north down 01 Left, the parallel runway is to the far right, which is shorter. I was cleared to land on the east/west taxiway between the two lakes in a 57 mph wind.
Photographer Randy Lippincott.

Turbulence comes in many forms and altitudes, such as mountain wave and clear air turbulence (CAT). We try to quantitate turbulence as occasional or continuous light chop, light, moderate, or severe. Like a ship on water, the ride changes with the weather.

Sometimes I had to deal with strong crosswinds during the critical phase of a touchdown. In the course of my early career, I was flying the Cessna 207 commercially when I was scheduled to land at the very barren and desolate Sheldon Point (in 1999 renamed Nunam Iqua–Yupik, meaning "end of the tundra") at the mouth of the Yukon River. The region was flatter than a pancake and treeless—an all-white wasteland on the Bering Sea. The wind virtually came off the water unimpeded. I listened and watched as a much larger, heavier, well-equipped turbine airplane ahead of me made several failed approaches and was unable to land due to the stiff crosswind. Thankfully, from day one in Nebraska, my training included crosswind landings. Somehow, I intuitively knew what to do and how to fly the airplane in this situation. It was a typical reflexive response, something I did not honestly have to think about; for me, it was just another one of those times. I waited for the Cessna Caravan to depart the area and then started my approach on the snow packed wilderness runway. Yes, I was crabbing sideways on my arrival, but straightened out the airplane on touchdown, dipped the upwind wing, and uneventfully rolled out to the end of the runway. My company agent was waiting there for me to pick up the mail as planned. We made the exchange, and in four minutes I was headed back into the air, never thinking anything unusual had just happened.

However, previously on June 7, 1989, a Canadian Bellanca Super Viking crashed. That day, there was a strong wind out of the south that caused a severe downdraft as they approached the mountain saddle. The pilot had attempted to fly over the ridge at a right angle. When he realized that he did not have adequate altitude to cross safely, he initiated a hard left turn. At cruising speed, the radius of the turn was large enough that it was already too late to avoid the nearby rocky face. It was all over in a few terrorizing seconds; it's called CFIT by the NTSB. It was the recurring Alaskan mountain tragedy. The pilot should have approached the ridge at a 45 degree angle; then, if a downdraft caused an unsafe condition, he could quickly and safely turn away, even at high speeds.

The passengers were reported missing, but the ELT was so seriously damaged during the accident that it was not working properly. Once the wreckage was located 100 miles south of Fairbanks in the Alaska Range, the Alaskan Alpine Club was called on to initiate the body recovery. As mountain rescue volunteers, Mark Wumkes and I were inserted by an Alaska State Trooper using a Bell Jet Ranger. As part of that team, the helicopter dropped us off near the crash site, and it did not take long to climb to the wreckage and survey the solemn remains.

For me, it was a somber memorial for the three young people who patiently waited for us to return their bodies to the waiting families. I shall always vividly recall the details of the mostly intact, but inverted aircraft that faced downhill. The silent wreck settled at the end of a long trail plowed in the snow that led back to the impact site on the stone face far above. It told a harrowing story in one melancholy glance. We had not been there long when we endured a nearby and dangerous soft slab avalanche. After identification had been made, we assumed a defensive posture to avoid further fatalities in the exposed and tenuous setting.

The *Sitka Daily Sentinel* reported: Warm weather and avalanches have prevented rescue workers from recovering the bodies of three people killed in a plane crash in the Alaska Range early this week. The Alaska State Troopers said the bodies of David A. Evans (ironically his stage name was Peregrine), 34, of Winnipeg, Manitoba; his brother, Meirig Evans, 18, of Ottawa, Ontario; and Patricia Olalde, 22, of Miami, Florida, could remain on the isolated mountain 100 miles south of Fairbanks for awhile. They were aboard a light plane that crashed Monday. "We're taking it very slow and easy," said 1st Sgt. Drew Rotermund. "It may take days, and it may take weeks to get them out of there. On Wednesday, an avalanche passed within 100 feet of rescue mountaineers while they were at the crash site." The Evans brothers were on a three-week tour of Alaska, according to their family in Canada. Rotermund said he did not know about the connection between Olalde, a student at the University of Louisville in Kentucky, and the two men. Rotermund said, "The climbing party removed enough personal possessions, such as checkbook, wallets, and notebooks, from the wreck to identify the three...."[15]

Patricia Olalde was a dancer and choreographer with the Louisville Ballet, who was acclaimed nationally for her dance works. She was the daughter of an English mother and a French-Basque father born in Santurce, Puerto Rico. Though Olalde was an accomplished dancer, her real gift was choreography, which revealed an engaging and provocative talent. Later I wrote to family members about my role in the recovery and my ardent personal grief for the survivors. I replayed in my mind what it must have been like those final moments. Did they have any last words or were they numbed with fear and unable to speak. There was no suffering; it was a mistake that was over in a split second. The trip of a lifetime interrupted by a lifetime's passage.

---

[15] AP page 8, *Sitka Daily Sentinel*, Sitka, Alaska, Friday, June 16, 1989.

Fire—Avoid the Pyroclastic Surge at All Costs

That first summer with Larry's Flying Service I flew all single-engine equipment. I piloted the Cessna 207 and the slippery Piper Saratoga with retractable gear. I enjoyed the Saratoga and appreciated its speed. My assignment that day was the mail run to the village of Beaver on the Yukon, just upriver from Stevens Village. I leveled off at 9,500 feet over the White Mountains when I throttled back for cruise flight. Immediately, I sensed that something was not right; the engine seemed to be running increasingly irregular. At that juncture, I was well beyond the point-of-no-return, and there were no airports nearby. I switched tanks thinking the problem was possibly contaminated fuel; I checked the mags and electric fuel pump—negative, they were all okay. Next, I adjusted the throttle and mixture settings until the roughness disappeared. It reminded me of my much more remote episode over the Alaska Range in the Cessna 205 where my cool head prevailed.

Following the power adjustment, I was unable to maintain altitude and slowly started a descent. My intention was to make it all the way to Beaver with the power setting that seemed to work, and I didn't want to touch anything. I simply had no idea what was askew with the engine, but I didn't like it. Fortunately, all the gauges stayed in the green and no oil sprayed on the windscreen. I made an uneventful landing and was greeted by the local agent. He gave me a ride to the village where I notified the company of my situation. I didn't have to wait long for a Frontier Flight to land, and I flew back to Fairbanks with the competition.

That afternoon, Timber, the mechanic, did some troubleshooting on the Saratoga, and it didn't take long to identify the problem. He had recently worked on the fuel injectors and had failed to tighten them when he finished. If even one fuel injector had vibrated loose, it would have sprayed fuel over the hot exhaust, erupting into flames. I would have been cremated alive in the resulting fireball over the White Mountains. I didn't appreciate being a test pilot because I certainly wasn't getting paid like one.

Accidental fires come in many forms. During a stop in Ambler, I was witness to the recent aftermath of an accidental ground aircraft fire. The outline of the black ash against the surrounding white snow was in the perfect shape of an airplane. The charred debris, which had been the powerful engine, was a slightly larger smoldering mound contrasted by the bordering snow. In random areas, were small "pools" of aluminum that had collected; there were ingots of the lightweight metal, remnants of what had been a sophisticated flying machine. I understood from the locals that the airplane had been "plugged in," just like I had plugged my airplane in so many times. We will never know if it was a frayed wire, an innocent short, or a negligently overloaded extension cord. From that day, every time I connected my personal airplane to power, I envisioned that charred tangle of wreckage neatly outlined on the ground where a sophisticated aircraft had once been parked. I retrieved one of those chunks of aluminum and have it on my desk today as a reminder of that unattended electrical accident.

Strike One

I always thought that I'd feel different when struck by lightning, but I didn't. On June 25, 1992, flight #136 to Galena, Alaska, in a PA 31-350, I was IFR cruising at 10,000 feet with eight passengers. I throttled back to maneuvering speed for safety and was ready to penetrate some totally benign-looking vertical development in the fluffy white clouds. I was also monitoring the AM radio for static to determine the frequency and magnitude of any nearby lightning. The reported serious cumulonimbus buildups were forecast to be well south of my route. However, I was not equipped with onboard weather radar or lightning detection, but that was standard procedure for northern operations.

There was light to moderate turbulence in the clouds when the static started to build on the radio until all reception was momentarily blocked and the radio went silent. The static faded several times, and then the flash occurred. I was hand flying the Chieftain because I didn't want to overload the autopilot in turbulent weather. Lightning struck the nose cone while I was looking directly at it. A spray of sparks erupted in front of the right windscreen between the fuselage and the propeller, all less than a few feet from where I sat. I didn't register a loud boom or dramatic flash due to the extreme brightness of the cloud layer and my dark sunglasses. In retrospect, my response was completely stoic and objective. As captain of the turbocharged twin-engine airplane, I had to remain in control of the situation, as well as the aircraft. My passengers, on the other hand, were very vocal in their reaction to the dramatic event. Their cries of fear and shrieks of terror were the most disconcerting things to me. I could not be distracted! My focus was first to fly the airplane and assess the situation.

If the plane was on fire, or both of my engines stopped, I quickly calculated that the only legitimate emergency alternate landing site was in nearby Ruby, and I thought about diverting. I had plenty of altitude to get there, just across the Yukon River. I waited for changes in my instrumentation or flight control inputs; nothing happened. Sully had not landed in the Hudson yet, but I knew that there was no way that I was going to land this airplane in the mighty Yukon River with eight passengers and no life-vests.

My next sensory input was from a sharp, acrid odor (ozone) that immediately filled the cabin. I anxiously waited for smoke and flames to follow the smell of the electrical burn, but it didn't materialize. Quickly, I reviewed the in-flight fire procedures and located the fire extinguisher. In a few minutes, the cabin air cleared and all navigation and engine readings remained normal. My secondary reaction was regarding my personal GPS. The global positioning system was drawing electricity from the Navajo, and a potential subsequent strike could fry the expensive compact unit. I immediately noted my time and distance to my destination and the nearby emergency runway. Next, I switched it off and disconnected the power source. I did not declare an emergency but requested priority handling, in no uncertain terms, with the Galena Tower. We had bounced around awhile longer before we were in the clear and it was time to begin our descent. I started to breathe easier as I powered back with the field in sight.

After landing, the damage survey proved to be minimal, but maintenance grounded the aircraft for a new propeller, and an engine tear down as directed by the respective manufacturers. They found multiple small burns on the nose skin along with surprisingly small weld-like burns on each of the three propeller blades from the 20,000° temperature generated by the lightning. There was a two-inch charred exit hole on the upper tip of the tail. I was assigned the job to ferry the plane back to Fairbanks—without passengers. Just another day in the bush for an astraphobic.

Occasionally, airline pilots report an unusual discharge called an "up flash." Lightning may occur between large storms and in the clear air above, possibly caused by electrons cascading down from the ionosphere. Massive cumulonimbus clouds are the most typical sources of lightning, but it is also generated by cumulus, stratus, and other kinds of clouds. These include snowstorms, sandstorms, and clouds over erupting volcanoes, all found in Alaska. Lightning can occur in the clear air within a few miles of a thunderstorm. However, more than half of all discharges occur within a cloud. The remainder takes place between clouds and the ground, with occasional cloud-to-cloud or cloud-to-air discharges.

At any one time, about 2,000 thunderstorms may exist worldwide, producing lightning flashes at a total rate of 100 per second. In an average year, about fifty people are killed and several hundred injured by lightning strikes in the United States. This mortality rate is less than from floods or tornadoes. Total property losses due to lightning in the United States range as high as several hundred million dollars per year. Lightning also causes an estimated 10,000 forest fires annually. Most fires in Alaska burn unattended unless they threaten personal property. During my time in Alaska, three million acres of forest burned every year, mostly due to natural causes.

Ball lightning, a little-understood phenomenon, is spherical, from 0.4 to more than 40 inches in diameter. It usually lasts less than five seconds. The lightning balls are reported to move horizontally at speeds of a few yards per second and then decay silently or with a small explosion. Many things in life are unpredictable, and I am sure that lightning is one of them. I discovered that truth at 10,000 feet over the unpopulated expanses of Alaska. That substantiates the theorem proposed by the immortal words of SNL's Roseanne Rosanna Dana's father; "It just goes to show, you never can tell."

During 1989, the Redoubt Volcano erupted and spread ash over Anchorage, Alaska. It also caused an emergency on KLM Flight 867 when all four engines flamed out as they flew through the ash while enroute to Tokyo from Amsterdam. The jumbo airliner descended from 25,000 feet to 12,000 feet in eight minutes before the crew was able to restart two of the engines, but all four were operating when the plane made an emergency landing in Anchorage.

In 1992, I was the first to land in Anchorage after the city was showered with ash from the Mount Spurr volcano from 80 miles to the west. Fortunately, Anchorage was far enough away from the source to avoid the pyroclastic surge. I flew the ABC film crew into Merrill Field downtown after the city had been closed due to the toxic and abrasive fallout from the volcano. I got the short straw when I was entrusted with the "disposable" twin-engine Aztec. The airplane wasn't as aesthetically pleasing as the Chieftain but was reliable and functional. Being on assignment with a major network TV crew was exciting. The flight down to the sight of the volcanic fallout was perfect. When I overflew the downtown field before landing, it reminded me of the drab Soviet Block cities I'd seen in Eastern Germany. Everything was covered with two inches of a flat gunmetal gray extremely fine powder; all color was systematically camouflaged.

Earlier, midday darkness from the volcano had fallen over the city, enough to cause the street lights to come on during the active fallout period. However, it had cleared in time for my trip. Once I landed at Merrill Field and rolled out to where I imagined the tarmac was and shut down, it was strangely quiet. There was no evidence of human activity. When I stepped off the airplane, it was easy to see my tracks anywhere that I walked. It reminded me of footage of the moon landing. The choking ash covered everything and was easily disturbed. It quickly went from a novelty to a real pain. I'm glad that I wasn't going to have to clean up that mess or be there when it rained. I deposited the film crew and departed the "ghost town" for Fairbanks. As I taxied out, I was careful to turn away from the crew and not blast them in a cloud of airborne ash. Engine start and initiation of aircraft movement were the only risky periods of sucking ash into the motors. It was odd not to see anyone on the streets, and even more unnatural not to see or hear anyone in the air on the radio in the largest city in Alaska. For me, it was a once in a lifetime event.

Coldfoot Jeep Commercial

Coldfoot is the jumping off place for Gates of the Arctic, with a population of ten at the 2010 census. It primarily serves as a truck stop on the Dalton Highway (the Haul Road) from Fairbanks to Galbraith Lake and Prudhoe Bay. Coldfoot was definitely in the middle of "fly-over country," and I made a mental note of it many times on the way to Deadhorse from Fairbanks. But I never had a reason to land there until I delivered the film crew for a Jeep commercial. The Chieftain was at its weight limit by the time passengers, bags, and filming paraphernalia was loaded. Coldfoot was a remote location—and it was cold! I'm sure the commercial turned out famously for the ubiquitous 4-wheel drive. Of course, I just dropped the crew off. I had no idea if the objects of the "shoot" had even been delivered.

However, to keep my own foot from getting cold, I wore "Bunny Boots" every day, all winter long. The white Bunny Boot was designed for cold, dry weather applications. A byproduct of the Korean war, they were inexpensive, came in all sizes, and were readily available. Each rubber boot had a small air valve in the upper lateral portion as an integral part of the efficient pneumatic insulation. At altitude, the boot would expand and could impair circulation to the foot. At that point, I would twist open the little valve and quickly release the pressure. They fit perfectly and kept my feet warm and safe during my long working days in the extreme environment.

My Trifecta

The *coup de grâce* for me was a three day weekend of extreme flying in northern Alaska: extremely north to the Barrow Wiley Post/ Will Rogers Memorial Airport on the Chukchi Sea; extremely east to

Eagle on the Yukon River and the Canadian border; and extremely west to the remote beaches of Wales, Alaska, on the Bering Sea. In three consecutive days, I flew to the most northern, most eastern, and the most western settlements on mainland Alaska north of the Alaska Range; it was officially my "old stomping grounds."

On Friday, my task was to pick up eight convicts and a single guard in Barrow with the Chieftain workhorse. Overall they were good passengers; they stayed in their seats, didn't try to escape, but were lousy tippers. I was not carrying a gun at the time of the 436 nautical mile scenic flight back to Fairbanks where the state troopers were waiting for me on the ramp.

Barrow (name changed to Utqiaġvik in 2016) is 320 miles north of the Arctic Circle and is among the oldest permanent settlements in the United States. The native Iñupiat lived around Barrow as far back as AD 500. Today it has a thriving population of over 4,000. West and north of Deadhorse, Alaska, Barrow was significantly influenced by the vast oil fields on the North Slope. One of the more popular hangouts in Barrow was Pepe's North of the Border Restaurant. Unfortunately, this popular and famous Mexican landmark burned to the ground in 2016.

Saturday, my charter flight was only 171 nautical miles to Eagle, the sight of the chrome globe monument dedicated to Roald Amundsen, the first man to complete the voyage through the deadly and frozen Northwest Passage in 1906. He skied 500 miles overland from his winter camp on the Beaufort Sea to telegraph the news to the rest of the world. The Northwest Passage was a historic expedition that Joyce and I retraced over 28 days in 2015 as we followed Amundsen's route from east to west. Eagle is located where the Yukon River entered Alaska from Canada and was settled by indigenous peoples, including the Hän, a thousand years ago. The population was 86 at the 2010 census, and in February, Eagle hosts a checkpoint for the long-distance Yukon Quest Sled Dog Race. The record low ambient temperature recorded in January was -71° Fahrenheit.

On Sunday, the best had been saved for last when I was assigned to fly 509 nautical miles to historical Wales, Alaska, population 149. Wales became an important whaling center due to its location along migratory whale routes, but it was named after the country in Western Europe. The influenza epidemic from 1918 to 1919 decimated its population and economy. Wales is coastal with almost no tidal excursion on the Bering Straits. While my client attended a village meeting that morning, I tried to get some exercise and found myself on the seashore, beach combing. In a short distance, I discovered an immense bleached bowhead whale vertebrae discarded in the extremely fine white sand. It was massive, washed out, but almost entirely intact. I have it displayed in my library to this day. The remarkable scene while standing on the shore was that of Little and Big Diomede Island along with a clear view of the Russian coast. (No, Sarah Palin did not live there.) Wow! From that perspective, the notion of a land bridge did not seem all that improbable. The people who crossed the Bering Land Bridge 36-43,000 years ago lived a subsistence lifestyle and were the ancestors of the "Eskimo" people. Referred to as Beringia, the land bridge was 620 miles long and had a favorable mild climate at the time of their crossing. The Thule People who settled Greenland more than 3,000 years ago gained access through this same route.

During my travels, I became acutely aware of the history of dinosaurs in Alaska on the North Slope. I knew that there were many fossils in the 49th state and that the first petrified dinosaur remains were discovered there in 1961. Now, recent finds help draw an entirely new picture of the prehistoric beasts. Alaska's North Slope dinosaurs lived in places once thought impossible for dinosaurs to survive, or else the climate was much different then. The number of separate dinosaurs found on the Alaskan North Slope and the amounts of fossils recovered surpass all other dinosaur sites in the rest of the world's polar regions. Twelve known dinosaur types have been cataloged on the North Slope while evidence for a 13th is under review. All are about 68-73 million years old and are from the Late Cretaceous Period.

Previously, paleontologists assumed all dinosaurs were cold-blooded. Only in the 1960s, did scientists begin entertaining the possibility that dinosaurs could be warm-blooded? So far, no DNA has been found in dinosaur bones on the North Slope. No one knows the exact answers to the many questions about their previous existence in this area. However, new discoveries on the Colville River throw doubt on the migration theory. Several new dinosaur fossils, including small meat-eaters, probably could not physically migrate the round-trip distance of 5,000 miles. Instead, North Slope dinosaurs may have survived year-round on ancient river systems that supported lush summer vegetation. Enough seasonal plant life may have grown during the 24-hour sunny summers to last during the cool-to-cold dark days of winter. Major Alaskan dinosaur sites include the Colville River, Western North Slope, Talkeetna Mountains, and the Aniakchak National Park and Preserve on the Alaskan peninsula.

I look back on those days with exceptional fondness. As far as I was concerned, I had the best job on Earth. In a nutshell, I was paid to explore and sightsee and still slept in my own bed at night. It was everything that anyone could ask, including two completely separate mountain ranges with the tallest peak in North America, Mt. McKinley, at 20,320 feet. I discovered massive sand dunes, virgin rivers, grand evidence of glaciation, actual glaciers, volcanic calderas, meteor impact craters, and endless expanses of tundra. Yes, world class vistas, all types of wildlife, forests, wilderness as far as the eye could see; and it was all mostly unspoiled by man. There were isolated areas of historic gold mining regions with intact dredges from the early 1900s. Visible from the air was the 800 miles of the historic 48-inch Alaskan Pipeline and coastal remnants of the Distant Early Warning System (DEW Line sites) that were evidence of the cold war. There were millions of lakes and large swift rivers. Then there were the native people; I admired the "Bush People" who lived a subsistence lifestyle in an unforgiving environment. I envied their way of living, in tune with nature, and mostly self-sufficient.

It Was Well Over 100 Feet

Sunday was my day off, and it was about one o'clock in the afternoon when my boss Larry called. I was the only man available, and he needed someone to take a last minute charter downriver to

Ruby. I told him that normally I would be happy to, but I had already had a drink that day. He wanted to know exactly how much I had consumed. I told him truthfully that it was a single beer, but I was uncomfortable with that, and I knew that the law prohibited any drinking. At that point, he said that a single beer didn't count, and I should take the charter flight as a favor to him. I tried to resist, but it was no use. He needed me. The evening charter flight was for the Silver Dollar Award at the village of Ruby on the famous Iditarod Trail. It was a mid-point prize for the first sled dog team to reach Ruby, and it was fly now or lose the exclusive charter. "First To The Yukon" award was sponsored by the Millennium Alaskan Hotel. The lucky winner earned a fantastic five-course meal created by the Millennium's Head Chef. The first one to the designated checkpoint that year got $500 in silver coins, and a catered white table cloth, sit-down, formal, five-course dinner. My passengers included the chef, sous-chef, and all the ingredients for a black-tie gourmet meal. There were crates of dishes, pots and pans, linen, crystal, and Dom Pérignon on ice for the exquisite feast. The beer morning had turned into a champagne flight for the elegant evening.

As it turned out, I acquiesced to the pressure from my employer. I can say that it was the only time in 50 years that I had piloted anything with even a trace of alcohol in my blood. The image of the Exxon Valdez on Bligh Reef flashed through my mind. The Federal law in the contiguous United States is that you're supposed to wait eight hours to fly. The saying goes, "Eight hours from bottle to throttle." In Alaska, the hilarious deviation is that it's not eight hours, but rather, "100 feet." After all that, it came true for me that day.

In 2017, the Iditarod came through Fairbanks due to the lack of snow on the southern portions of the trail. Usually, the endurance race doesn't go through Ruby every year. The route is supposed to take a southern trail on odd years. The first trek was made in 1925 because of an epidemic of diphtheria. The children of Nome desperately needed the serum to survive the winter. The daring sled dog relay through the harsh Alaskan winter and the open terrain was to deliver life-saving medicine to the small village of Nome. The original "Great Race of Mercy" involved 20 drivers and more than 150 dogs. Today it is commemorated annually by the Iditarod Trail Sled Dog Race. The main route of the Iditarod Trail extends 938 miles from Seward in the south to Nome in the northwest.

It was along this same historical trail, but minding my own business on a routine mail-run downriver at Kaltag, when it happened—and it was way before Sully Sullenberger's emergency landing on the Hudson River. The bird strike was a full-sized Raven that impacted the very top part of the windshield, but the flight was never in question. Unlike Sully, I intended to land. I was slowed down in the traffic pattern and had just turned onto my base leg when the impact came out of nowhere. Bam! It was over just like that. Luckily, it didn't shatter the $10,000 heated windshield on the Piper Navajo Chieftain. If I had been at cruise speed, the Raven most likely would have penetrated the windshield. Bird guts in the cabin is a gruesome sight, and I never planned to wear goggles! I was glad to get that once-in-a-lifetime experience out of the way. Blessed to have been in a landing configuration and NOT taking off over the mighty Yukon River, my outcome may have been much more like Sully's. Ravens tend to gather near villages as they are scavenger birds and can be annoying, particularly around the dump when it is near the airport. There was nothing for me to do except continue working (I had a schedule to keep) and there was no statistical reporting to the Feds.

I had one "near runway incursion" during my entire professional flying career. Otherwise, I had no opportunity to talk to the Feds other than some friendly impromptu ramp checks. An incursion is when there are two aircraft on the runway at the same time. One aircraft has permission, and one does not. That day, carrying eight passengers, I was taxiing westbound at Fairbanks International. I was cleared by ground control to cross 1-9 left and then 1-9 right, for a 1-9 right full-length departure per our company protocol. I followed ground control's instructions, including complete and accurate read-backs. While crossing 1-9 right, out of habit, I glanced at the departure end of the runway and saw an Alaska Airlines 737 jet accelerating toward me. There was no real danger as the jet was still 5,000 feet down the runway, but it was clear that somebody goofed. The FAA tried to put the onus on me and charged me with a runway incursion.

Following the review of the official tower tapes, I was acquitted of any wrongdoing. I had indeed been authorized to cross 1-9 right by the ground control while the tower operator had simultaneously cleared the 737 to depart. This time, the human error was in the tower and not my cockpit.

During those protracted weeks of investigation, I relearned a valuable lesson while suffering considerable angst—after all, this was my livelihood. The lesson was to fill out an Aviation Safety Reporting System (ASRS) report any time even a potential violation occurred (occasionally referred to as a NASA form). If the confession was complete and non-criminal in nature, it guaranteed full immunity from prosecution. The Aviation Safety Reporting System was in place for learning and a one time, get-out-of-jail-free card. The trick was that the report must be submitted within 14 days of the violation; and if used to insulate the individual from prosecution, then the clock would be reset for infractions but only after two years had lapsed. I was a member of the Aircraft Owners and Pilots Association (AOPA) legal assistance program. My first call was to them, and they gave me the legal advice that I needed to maintain my flying profession.

Along with the increased responsibilities of the ATP license, came a requirement for a flight physical every six months and a company IFR checkride. I remember that the checkride in the Chieftain was stressful for me at first. There were a lot of things to do, correctly, the first time. I did not take the job lightly. It was the only time that I ever had the opportunity to practice emergency single engine procedures. I vividly remember flying the ILS and over-gripping the control wheel; yes, I could feel beads of sweat coming out on my forehead. It was intense work, my focus was fueled with adrenaline, and I knew my job hinged on it. Eventually, I overcame the white-knuckle IFR checkride to ATP standards and grew very comfortable with the Navajo "flying truck."

Now, some might say that I was too comfortable flying in Alaska. Weather reports were not always reliable in the expanse of the great Alaskan interior (my lightning encounter is an example). I typically was assigned Kotzebue as my west coast destination for the day in the Chieftain. Sometimes, there would be an intermediate stop on the way to the coast. Since we commonly flew at 10-11,000 feet enroute, occasionally I would be on top of a cloud deck when I arrived near the intermediate destination. These remote villages did not have instrument approaches or the possibility of radio contact with ATC. Because I flew the same trip every day, I was familiar with the terrain and over time designed my personal instrument arrival procedures along with safe minimum descent altitudes. Since my life depended on this, I did not take the task lightly or cut any corners. These were self-designed early day global positioning system (GPS) IFR approaches in the Alaskan wilderness. It was not until December 1993 that GPS achieved initial operational capability (IOC), the month after I moved away from Alaska. Even with GPS as a backup, the workload for the IFR single-pilot could be very busy and stressful. There was no one to consult or double check your life and death calculations and no radar to verify your position. The counterpoint was that there could be no miscommunication with your first officer (co-pilot).

Water for Ice

Airframe icing can be the pilot's worst nightmare. It can come in the form of clear, rime, or mixed ice. Ice builds on the leading edges of the airplane that first impacts the air. The hard-water buildup quickly changes the form, function, and weight of the aircraft. Virtually all bets are off; its formation and progress are predictably unpredictable. The speed at which ice can build up can be surprising. The airplane has to carry the additional weight, and along with the altered (or rather experimental) wing shape can cause your aircraft to lose lift and possibly crash. Icing is particularly critical close to the ground. I have personally experienced every type of ice both day and night.

Ice does not come out of the clear sky. You must be flying in visible moisture (clouds or rain) for ice to form. The astute pilot turns on all anti-icing equipment before entering conditions even remotely susceptible to icing. Icing may occur typically when the outside air temperature (OAT) is between 32° and -4° Fahrenheit, but the most severe icing will usually occur between 32° and 14° Fahrenheit. If the temperature/dew point spread is fewer than 2° Fahrenheit and the temperatures are freezing, one must be especially vigilant for ice. I also learned that the most aggressive icing is encountered in the top 1,000 feet of cumulus clouds. Normally the freezing level was at the ground in Alaska, but I always kept an eye on the OAT gauge. Average operating air temperatures aloft seemed to be around -45° Fahrenheit. At that temperature, the air is unable to retain much, if any, moisture. Counterintuitively, in the extremely cold temperatures, ice is unlikely; the frigid air can hold little moisture. The rules are that you should climb through potential icing as quickly as possible, and delay descents for landing as long as it is safe when icing temperatures and visible moisture surround an airport.

Flying from Anchorage to Fairbanks in my Skyhawk; I was low-level, due to the cloud cover over the Parks Highway just north of Talkeetna, when suddenly and unexpectedly I flew into severe weather. Clear ice is freezing rain, super-cooled water droplets that freeze upon contact. The most dramatic encounter is clear ice, as it can cover the largest area of the airplane the fastest and can be the most deadly. Instantly, my windshield glazed over and became opaque. The leading edge of the wing was quickly and dramatically building ice, and I could see transparent ominous tentacles actively growing, reaching back well under the leading edge of the wings. The ice was changing shape as I watched. I had to maneuver the airplane low-level while looking out the side window—the same way Lindbergh flew across the Atlantic. Immediately I recognized the grave situation that I was in and initiated an 180 degree turn and applied maximum carburetor and pitot heat; all bets were off. There was NO consideration of continuing in the obviously dangerous and futile conditions. I hung around for better weather after safely landing in Talkeetna where I proceeded to remove the buildup of ice from the trusty 172, and waited for it to melt off of the windshield. Recognition of the problem and quick action is the only thing that saved me that day.

I was flying a Ryan Air 207 at night from Buckland to Kotzebue when I first experienced the innocent looking, slow growing "Styrofoam" called rime ice, form on my wings and struts. Over open water with minimum forward visibility, I could see down in the darkness that I was in and out of low lying clouds. The temperature was well below 32° Fahrenheit. The icing was a gradual process, and I could monitor the rime ice with my flashlight looking out the side window at the leading edge of the Cessna's large wing. At first, I noticed the change when the windshield turned white. The ice was smooth, homogeneous, opaque, and milky white. After landing in Kotzebue, again looking out the side window, I used a broomstick and glycol to remove any evidence of the unfortunate encounter. Ice will only form in freezing conditions and in the presence of visible moisture, like clouds or rain. If you pass through clouds on your climb-out, any acquired ice will sublimate in clear air over a short period. It is prudent to monitor your OAT and know exactly where the freezing level is. If you pick up unmanageable ice on a cross country trip, descent through the freezing level may be your last best option to shed or melt the ice.

One day in the Chieftain I ran into my most dramatic and worrisome mixed icing encounter. I was flying at 7,000 feet in the clouds when suddenly I started to pick up mixed ice. It was an oddly cobbled and ugly combination of both clear and rime icing. It looked different than anything I had ever seen. Equipped for known-icing, the Navajo usually handles this as a non-event. I watched the wings and waited until I had about three-quarters of an inch of ice and popped the pneumatic boots. If the rubber boots were inflated prematurely, it would create room under the thin plastic ice. Subsequently, it would become impossible to remove it from the wing, as new ice would accumulate outside the "artificial space." If correctly timed, the thicker more brittle ice broke off with the first inflation. However, this time, almost as quickly, the boots were covered in more of the extremely aggressive ice. Immediately, I recognized the urgency of the situation. This scenario was dramatic and something that I had never experienced before. Without immediate action on my part, there was no doubt that a crash was likely to follow.

At this point, I could go up, or I could go down. While popping the boots, I quickly started a max power climb to a greater height and notified ATC of my situation. Remember: first aviate, next navigate, then communicate when you have taken care of the priorities. With more altitude come more options, and, therefore, increased safety. I could tell that this situation called for swift action. The caveat was that aggressive climbing exposes the bottom of the wing, and this can be a critical mistake causing additional ice to accumulate well outside the region of the rubber boots on the underside of the wing. I was inflating the boots every ten to fifteen seconds, and the rate of buildup was dramatic and unprecedented. Then, I was greatly relieved that suddenly I climbed out of the life-threatening icing conditions. The flight was never truly in question, but the encounter surely got my attention.

Up the River

Although uneventful, the trip in August of 1993 was indelibly etched in my mind. It was the finest Alaskan afternoon, and the marvel of fall in the Arctic was about to unfold for me. As a temporary company check airman, I was assigned to give our new chief pilot en-route training in the old twin-engine Aztec. The first leg of our trip was routine and filled with cockpit chatter. We hashed over changes taking place in our organization and other aviation related business. The weather was clear and the visibility unrestricted. Craig climbed to 6,500 feet for a smooth ride on the mail run into Allakaket. He made a heading correction as we passed upstream from Rampart and crossed the Yukon River. In a short time, we started our descent over "Crater Lake" as the Kanuti River Basin came into view. A brief discussion ensued regarding the crater's etiology and other known meteor craters in North America. The meteorite debate evoked the imagination of what the prehistoric cataclysmic event must have caused. It would have been a remarkable natural catastrophe witnessed hundreds of miles distant from ground zero.

The vast Alaskan interior concealed any signs of man until we reached our first stop on the Koyukuk River. We overflew the native village and landed on the gravel runway that paralleled the river. Met by our indigenous agent, we delivered the mail in short time, and we were on our way upriver to Bettles. Established in 1899, it was a predominantly white mining settlement, 35 miles north of the Arctic Circle. The low-level excursion up the John River started 15 miles northwest of Bettles. As we entered a broad canyon, the magic of the Brooks mountain range began to unfold. Each new vista revealed a spectacular rainbow of brilliant colors. The bright blue sky was punctuated with widely scattered fluffy white clouds that guarded only the tallest peaks. The abundant sunshine flooded the landscape and was absorbed as if the tundra knew of the imminent shortage. The primordial glacial valleys were quilted with brilliant tundra colors and appliqués of pine and tiny deciduous trees for texture. The vegetation reflected natural arctic geometric patterns in the underlying rock and soil. Later, I discussed the unusually vivid colors I had witnessed with an old timer. He verified that years of rare moisture and temperature combination would produce exceptionally resplendent colors in the Arctic. Graced by the unique visual phenomenon, I was busy cataloging each new scene before me.

The northern latitude linear formations, primarily hexagonal or honeycomb-like designs on the boggy canyon floor, were caused by the perennial freeze-thaw cycles over the millennia. Even for the casual observer, the signature Arctic patterns were striking and unique. During August, the sharp drop in temperature prompts the flora to burst with color in protest, as if committing suicide instead of dying the slow natural death of autumn. Today's range of light illuminated different shades of the Scarlet Red Tea Leaf Bush, whose exact pigment intensity and texture depended on its slope aspect and quality of the underlying soil. The vibrant nearly iridescent reds, contrasting greens, and yellows were bordered by the flat grays and browns of the proud distinctive rocky spires. The stark, barren crags, in turn, were crowned with termination dust (the first virgin snow of the coming season).

Approximately 30 nautical miles northwest of Bettles on the John River is the northernmost homestead. A Cessna 185 was smartly parked along the homemade runway on Crevice Creek. Many times when I have flown by, the pioneers gave me a hardy wave if they were outside hanging laundry or working in the neatly tilled garden. Although the isolated outpost is unforgiving in the winter, the summer melts away all the hardships and honestly seems like a paradise of amnesia. Oh, how I longed to live my next life right there on that parcel of land. It would be a spartan but incredibly rewarding existence.

A kaleidoscope for the traveler, the crispness of the day was augmented by remarkably shifting color schemes. The glacial-fed John River neatly divided the valley floor with a shimmering distinctly milky emerald green ribbon. Glaciers generate such enormous pressure on the rock that it produces extremely fine "flakey particles." Glacial flour or flocculated rock is easily held in suspension, which affects the refractive characteristic of the water. Crushed stone is granulated like sand on the beach, but the glacier pressure reduces the rock much like wheat is ground into flour by the millstone. Glacial flour in the melt water turns it into a distinctly milky turquoise color. No other function in nature produces a similar effect or unique shade.

Occasionally, one could detect the telltale sign of man in the overgrown footprint of an old winter trail that paralleled the river. As the valley twisted and turned, new color patterns sprang to life without fanfare; eventually, all trees gave way to the scrub willow. Anyone in Anaktuvuk Pass (translated, place of caribou droppings) must travel a considerable distance south to find any timber for logs. The distinctive and familiar towering peaks that bordered the quaint village of Anaktuvuk came into view, as the John River water cleared and withered closer to its source.

As Craig adjusted the throttles on the return flight, the faint odor of aviation fuel and oil drifted through the cabin of the well-used Aztec. I mentally studied local mountainous areas like the Arrigach and summits named Igipak, Gray Ghost, and Doonerak. These were remote places I fell in love with long before I ever saw the rugged peaks that filled the timeless landscape in a land far away from traditional civilization. I knew I was privileged to be a frequent witness; I also knew that one day it would only be a memory written on these lines.

My last commercial flight was in the PA-31-350, N222CC. The uneventful flight was down the Yukon River to Tanana and Galena, then on to Kaltag, Nulato, Koyukuk, and back to Fairbanks with passengers. It was a total of 4.4 flight hours and was most likely a

12 hour work day for me. That was it. I turned in my flight logs and my last time sheet, gave the company my forwarding address to send the check, and walked out the door. No fanfare, no cake, no farewell party. It had just been a job. But it was an occupation that I loved and that I looked forward to tackling each day. That work gave me exceptional piloting opportunities and challenges, but much more than that, it gave me a front seat to the greatest show on earth. I was up close and personal to severe and perfect weather, wildlife, the full spectrum of geology, and an opportunity to observe the native culture from the inside. It was an exciting job, and an education all rolled into one.

White-Knuckles for Whitehorse

Reluctantly, my aviation career had come to a close in November 1993. I headed to Arizona after I sold the house in Fairbanks and prepared to resume my profession as a Physician Assistant at Mayo Clinic in Scottsdale. My aviation career in Alaska had been shortened by my wife's desire to be closer to the family. Interviews with the airlines were fruitless because of my lack of turbine experience as well as a recent glut of military pilots. I had enjoyed the arduous rough-and-tumble calling as a "bush pilot" and was going to miss it. My logbooks reflected 5,000 hours of flight time in the previous four years. It was only three and a half years of active service, as I been off the job for six months with a work related ruptured lumbar disc. Now, maybe somewhat overconfident, I hopped in my little 172 and headed to Whitehorse, Yukon Territory, Canada, in the darkness through snow showers. My ultimate destination was Phoenix, Arizona, where my wife was already employed.

My brand-new Garmin 95 was a yoke-mounted GPS, and I used it as a supplemental navigation aid in the wilderness. It was a relatively long flight into Canada over a mostly inhospitable region. I was flying in and out of snow showers, but nothing was "sticking" to the wings, so I did not worry about icing. Soon enough I was able to pick up the Canadian VOR and contacted Whitehorse Approach on the radio in the bleak darkness. I had what I thought to be the Canadian airport entered in my GPS as a distance measuring equipment (DME) reference and back up. I had no idea that the 24 satellite system was not fully operational until two years later in 1995. My routine was to use the three letter designator for any aerodrome, but it was not the correct format for my new, untested international database. I foolhardily entered what I thought to be the identifier for the Whitehorse Airport and intended to fly to it through the murkiness. Little did I know that it was, in fact, the radio beacon (VOR) on top of the mountain north of the airport that I had entered, not the physical airport more than 5.8 nautical miles to the south. The Garmin only recognized the International Airport symbol as four letters. Three letters would only lead me into the rising terrain near the beacon—CFIT.

Left to right, Mark Wumkes, and Randy Lippincott.
Picture of a winter night time departure to Whitehorse in the Cessna 172.
Photographer unknown.

Out of habit, I had also set up the traditional instrument panel to fly the ILS at night in the snow-showers. In retrospect, I should have just filed an IFR flight plan, and that omission falls squarely into the arena of pilot error. Tired and at the end of a long day, I could have taken the shortcut of only looking at the Garmin and would have committed a fatal error. If I had done that, my flight path would have taken me directly into the side of the mountain where the VOR was strategically located and realized the dark fate of so many other aviators. Instead, I intuitively knew that things were not adding up, and I fell back on what I knew best. I learned a critical lesson: Do not rely on new equipment that I do not fully understand how to operate. It had been a brush with death flying "IFR" into Whitehorse on a night VFR flight plan. All of a sudden tomorrow didn't matter; it made me realize that I needed to live in the moment! Life honestly can be that fragile when the thin veil of the sky above intersects with the rocky terrain below.

PART FOUR
Arizona

I Was Cruising in Smooth Air...

The Ken Johnson Story

I was delighted to start my job in orthopedic surgery at Mayo Clinic in Scottsdale, Arizona. It was also wonderful to meet an experienced pilot who worked in the same department. His story and mine had so much in common that it was uncanny—especially the irrational justification of all things aviation. Ken Johnson was a physician in the Foot and Ankle Department and had over 2,000 hours of flight time. Soon after we met, he told me that he had a summer trip to Alaska planned for the following year. I was sure that we would have many stories to share. He had a new modified Piper Super Cub that he would be flying to the Arctic, and he planned to make a real adventure out of the trip. I was jealous and wanted to be on that trip but knew it was not feasible because I had no vacation time available. It was exciting to have someone to visit with about a shared passion, and I looked forward to flying with Ken in the little yellow Cub.

Saturday, December 4, 1993, after I had been at Mayo Clinic one month, the tragic word came in. I was shocked. I couldn't believe it. Ken suffered a fatal accident in his new Piper Cub along with a nurse who was his passenger. Soon after the crash, the stories started pouring in. People from Rochester, Minnesota, who knew Ken had plenty of tales to tell. That last and fatal wreck was his fifth off-airport landing. It seems that Ken had a horrible safety record, and a long history of poor judgment and bent airplanes. Sadly, he had paid the ultimate price for his caviler attitude toward the laws of aviation. I had been spared a painful confrontation that would have occurred at some point.

Later, I heard the tragic details: After Ken had breakfast in Payson that morning, he topped off all three tanks (including a new, untested belly tank) and was nearly 200 lbs. over maximum gross weight. Ken's history included stories of his typical low-level adventures. Apparently, he liked to fly close to the ground. This time, he flew up a box canyon and stalled the little airplane when he tried to make a forced last minute U-turn at gross weight. All the red flags were there, and they all caught up to him at once. Like my chief pilot in Alaska, he had an attitude of, "I'm a great pilot and don't need to follow those stupid rules, and I have survived just fine so far." Possibly, according to the NTSB report, the pivotal infraction was that narcotics were discovered in his system at the time of autopsy. The report indicated the improper use of prescription drugs while piloting an aircraft. I was thankful that I never had the opportunity to fly with him; I'm afraid that our different approaches to flying would have led to a serious conflict. I also modified my low-level personal antics somewhat after his death. My routine was to fly nap-of-the-earth only in a familiar area and then only down river or downhill. I have hedged my bets for the last half century.

In May 1994, a newspaper article reported an airplane crash on Roosevelt Lake, east of Phoenix. Two young people were in a 172 flying low-level over the lake in glassy water conditions. The first turn the pilot initiated over the reservoir resulted in clipping the surface with the left wingtip, which cartwheeled the plane into the lake. In the crash the young copilot and her seat were violently forced into the rear of the cabin; only the pilot was conscious and able to extricate himself as the aircraft sank. Flying close to any surface increases risk and decreases response time. Glassy water is the Venus flytrap for the unsuspecting aviator.

A Grand Flight

Not all flights begin at O'dark thirty, but it's a frequent occurrence in the deserts of Arizona. Up at 4:30 a.m., I checked the weather including the winds aloft—the best indicator of the flight's potential smoothness. The reports remained CAVU and the wind calm. With a minimal amount of packing, my passenger and I were off to the airport, coffee in hand. She was hesitant to overindulge in the caffeinated beverage, remembering the last lesson she had learned when we were unable to time our landing with her bladder.

The streets were empty on the drive to Falcon Field. I mentally reviewed the trip plans and equipment in the soothing darkness. Nodding to the bumps in the road, barely able to hold on to her coffee cup, my copilot was the reluctant tourist. Soon we were parked beside N65798. In the pre-dawn murk, we silently carried out the drill of loading and the preflight of the Cessna 172. In minutes, we were ready to push back and crank the Lycoming. Predictably, it came to life on the second revolution. I checked the oil pressure and switched on the avionics master. The GPS came to life, and I punched in our planned route: Falcon Field direct to Diamond Creek, where the sightseeing extravaganza would begin.

As we taxied to runway four right (4R), I listened to ATIS and made a call in the blind to the CTAF because the tower wasn't open yet. I followed the checklist and performed the run-up with robotic movements; all of the gauges were in the green, trim was set, we were ready for departure. I made one last call as I maneuvered the Skyhawk into position, adjusted the directional gyro (DG) on the runway heading, and applied power. The four-seater smoothly accelerated and we were airborne in a few seconds. I contacted Phoenix Departure and was cleared through Class Bravo Airspace in the Terminal Control Area (TCA). This request enabled us to continue our climb unrestricted as the sun's pre-dawn rays softly kissed the underside of the right wing good morning.

Floating above the fading sea of illumination, I identified the Scottsdale airport and surrounding main arteries. The glistening ocean of mercury lights melted with a blush of pink from desert and skyline and the engine's gyrating drone was making my eyelids heavy. I forced my eyes open and answered the handoff to Albuquerque Center. In no time, we leveled at our assigned VFR altitude in the silky-smooth air. I checked our ETA to Diamond Creek; we were ahead of schedule. It was time to relax, enjoy the scenery, and anticipate the truly fantastic vistas over the early morning Grand Canyon.

Arizona's topography is a diary of erosion. Contained in its pages is evidence of tectonic upheaval, land scoured by water, worn away by eons of relentless wind, and baked to overdone every day over the millennia. The early morning panoramas were breathtaking as pastels dissolved shadow in the shifting light. Each flaw in the land was bordered in peaceful black and gray as their outlines faded. Shades of green poked out of the fresh hues where there was evidence of precious moisture. Mountains, valleys, rivers, and mesas depicted on the aviation map sprang to life as we marveled from our lofty perch. The reflected sunlight from springs and ponds seemed to race with us, unimpeded across the rugged terrain, seemingly ready to pass me at any moment.

The Grand Canyon, located in northwestern Arizona, is a spectacular gorge carved by the Colorado River into rocks that represent an estimated two billion years of Earth history. Its total length from Lee's Ferry to Lake Mead is 277 miles. The canyon is more than one mile deep in places and is from 4 to 18 miles wide. Plateaus to the north and south rise 7,000 to 9,000 feet above sea level, partly as a result of regional uplift, which left the North Rim more than 1,000 feet higher than the South Rim in places. On the walls, strata of limestone, sandstone, lava, and other rocks are visible. Displaying various colors that evolve with the day, they are a featured attraction for the hordes of tourists who come to share the experience. Garcia-Lopez Cardenas, a Spanish explorer, "discovered" the canyon in 1540, but systematic exploration did not begin until 1850. Civil War veteran John Wesley Powell was the first to survey the canyon by boat in 1869. The Grand Canyon National Park, created in 1919, covers an area of 1.2 million acres.

Lured into complacency by the natural splendor of the territory, an inattentive aviator could become trapped in a box canyon, or blown off course by a summer storm, and run out of gas. Always, the double-edged sword looms overhead. The siren calls the novice airman to scurry hither and yon admiring all her brilliance, not realizing how fast the grains of sand run through the hourglass and the petrol through the carburetor. Arizona's harsh elements and vast interior, like Alaska, claims her fair share of the unwary or neophyte pilots each year.

Our direct route took us over Prescott, the site of the first territorial capital, formerly called Fort Whipple. It was part of the land north of the Gila River (pronounced Hee-La), acquired by annexation in 1850 following the Mexican-American War. White men did not appear for more than 10,000 years after the arrival of the Native American. The Grand Canyon State includes many diverse areas of majestic natural beauty and geological interest. The name was derived from the Pima Indian village of Arizonac (formerly located in what is now Mexico, near Nogales). The word Arizonac most likely means "place of the small spring," ironic that such a major river comprises a significant section of its border.

As we approached the Grand Canyon from the south, abeam the highest point in the state, Humphreys Peak (12,633 feet) near Flagstaff, the first hints of the canyon were vast mesas that abruptly ended in space. Gradually, more and more sharply expanding chasms merged into the mother of all canyons. From the air, I identified the railroad tracks that ran north of Williams. A refurbished old steam engine carries passengers back through time and space to the South Rim of the Grand Canyon. The first "easy access" to the Grand Canyon was from Williams in 1901 by rail for the price of $3.95. Today, through the effortless preprogrammed electronic guidance of GPS, I can sightsee with impunity.

The volcanic area between the San Francisco Peaks on the south and Kaibab Plateau on the north is referred to as the Coconino Plateau. The Kaibab and Coconino Plateaus ride atop the massive Colorado Plateau, which includes many of Utah's national parks to the north. The Colorado River divides the plateau, and its tributaries drain most of Arizona. This primary waterway flows for roughly 700 miles in the state, entering from the north, then winding westward (in part through the Grand Canyon) before turning south to form most of Arizona's western boundary. Just as in Alaska, where I completely traversed the Yukon River from Canada to the Bering Sea, I have also explored most of the Colorado River in Arizona. From the headwaters in the Rocky Mountains to the delta on the Sea of Cortez, each region has its extraordinary geography and unique history.

Our point of entry into the giant arc started at Diamond Creek, then upriver to the Grand Canyon Airport. The elementary splendor of "The Temple of The World" was revealed in Technicolor. We were privileged to witness the illusion referred to as a chasm. Busy cataloging the spectacular vistas of pinnacles, contrasting folded horizontal rock layers, blocky bluffs, lava flows, and teetering sandstone; we gazed straight down the massive sheer walls. I checked off landmarks like Cheops Pyramid, Wotan's Throne, and King Arthur's Castle. This eclectic "church" houses "temples" for Buddha, Brahma, Zoroaster, Confucius, and The Sanctuary of The Holy Grail. I identified formations like Apollo and Jupiter that were "out of this world."

Precisely, I steered from designated checkpoint-to-checkpoint vis-à-vis my "black box." I carefully followed the map to verify radio frequencies, position, and proper altitude. At appropriate intervals, I banked the aircraft for contrasting views behind us in the beautiful, enchanting light of early morning. This region is so captivating and photogenic, but I forgot to take even a single photograph. As the mighty Colorado River (the lowest point in the state on the river is seventy feet above sea level) zigzagged below our tiny craft, we caught occasional glimpses of river rafting parties docked on sandy beaches far below. I expect the boat people eagerly awaited the flood of the first warming rays of sunlight to reach the canyon floor.

The breathtaking beauty of this wonder overloads the faculties. The sheer scale is overwhelming, let alone the contrast of the relatively flat surrounding country to the perpendicular rocky ramparts. I was continuously drawn in a different direction to ensure that we did not overlook a more glorious spectacle. As I craned right and left, I wished the flight would never end. Below Supai Point, west of the Great Thumb Mesa, the Havasupai Indian land borders the park. A virtual oasis along Havasu Creek, the dense green vegetation was sprinkled with isolated small buildings and emerald ponds. No roads lead in or out; access is by foot alone.

Eager for yet another perfect canyon view, we approached the

Grand Canyon National Airport. I made all the necessary reporting calls, and permission was granted to enter the airport traffic area. Each year over four million visitors view the canyon; 400,000 of those tourists gaze at it from the air just as we were. An additional 40,000 hike the multiple trails leading down into the canyon. However, the aviator leaves no tracks, disturbs no natural scenery, and changes nothing for those who follow. I landed among the thick tall pine trees at the high-altitude airport on the South Rim. We taxied to the main terminal for fuel and directions to town. A short walk resulted in a hot breakfast and a good stretch.

An obscure man, Oliver Lippincott (not closely related to the author) was instrumental in opening the Grand Canyon to the masses. He had a greater impact than the Spanish explorer Cardenas, or the one-armed American, Powell, who first charted the course of the Colorado River through the "impenetrable canyon." On January 4, 1902, Lippincott arrived at the Grand Canyon. He was the first person to drive to the South Rim. In *The Story of Man at the Grand Canyon*, his long ago epic trip was described in detail. Lippincott navigated a gas-powered steam car (Toledo Eight-horse) from Flagstaff, Arizona, to the South Rim. Complicated by mechanical problems, it took him five days to reach his destination, but only seven hours for the return trip. In 1926, automobiles overtook the railroad as the most popular means to view the canyon.

Before departure from the Grand Canyon National Airport's 9,000-foot runway, I was careful to calculate the density altitude. As I retreated from the Colorado Plateau headed south, we were bordered to the east by the Painted Desert, an extensive area of colorful sand and rock formations. Further away was Canyon De Chelly (pronounced Canyon da Shay), with sheer red cliffs; the Petrified Forest, with great "logs" of jasper and agate; and Monument Valley (along the Utah border), surrounded by monolithic red sandstone buttes 1,000 feet high.

As we continued our climb, the oldest regional airfield, but the latest to be renovated, Grand Canyon Valle Airport (pronounced Valle'y) passed under the right wing. Originally built by TWA in 1940, it supplied all the air transport to the greater Grand Canyon area until the Grand Canyon National Airport opened in 1967. The first flight initiated these skies in 1921. The golden age of aviation was ushered in by Ford Trimotors, Stearmans, Howards, Staggerwing Beeches, and the Spartan Executive. Today, many of them reside at Valle Airport in "The Planes of Fame Museum."

After climbing to our cruising altitude, we enjoyed an endless view. The chilly air coming through the vents made for a welcome contrast with the warm sun on my chest. We were above the bases of widely scattered fair weather cumulus clouds in the tranquil air. In the distance loomed the threat of an afternoon thunderstorm. The indistinct distant horizon lay in a muted blue smoky haze, and a mixture of light reflected off the red sand. The cloud shadows played with mountaintops and desert alike. Occasionally the landscape was artificially divided by jeep trails, power lines, or a highway. Dry lakebeds contrasted with the sparsely forested mountainous country. Sometimes, when the angle was right, a flash of light was reflected off a moving car or small body of water. We could easily identify landmarks as far away as 100 miles.

As we neared Phoenix, I spotted the expansive Theodore Roosevelt Lake on the Salt River in the distance, as well as Bartlett and Horseshoe Reservoirs on the Verde River. Then Four Peaks was well defined as it became visible on the horizon. As an astute traveler, I was able to identify subtle burn areas. Miles of charred desert were vivid reminders of the volatile combination of dry climate and lightning. As we descended into the Phoenix valley, all the familiar local landmarks came into view: Weaver's Needle and Superstition Mountain, the McDowells, Red Mountain, South Mountain, and finally Camelback. Even closer, I spied the 330-foot fountain at Fountain Hills (still in the world's top five).

As I descended out of 7,000 feet near the Fort McDowell Bald Eagle Breeding Area, I detected an object in my peripheral vision. About 25 yards off my starboard, an eagle was in a dive parallel to my glide path. I didn't pass him all that quickly; he wouldn't deviate or even glance at me. Indeed, a cocky young bird of prey, he was out to prove that, no kidding, he had "The Right Stuff," and I was the one encroaching on his turf. I dialed in and listened to ATIS, and then received landing instructions from the Falcon Field Control Tower. As I pulled up to the fueling area to service the Skyhawk before parking, I noticed it wasn't even 10:00 a.m. Our flight time round-trip from Mesa was a total of four hours. Effortlessly, we had traversed two billion years of time and circumnavigated a third of the entire state that morning.

The naturalist John Muir described the Grand Canyon in the following way:

> It seems a gigantic statement for even Nature to make all in one mighty stone word. Wildness so God-full, cosmic, primeval, bestows a new sense of Earth's beauty and size. But the colors—the living, rejoicing colors, chanting morning and evening, in a chorus to heaven! Whose brush or pencil, however lovingly inspired, can give you these? In the Supreme flaming glory of sunset, the whole Canyon is transfigured, as if all the life and light of centuries of sunshine stored up in the rocks was now being poured forth as from one glorious fountain, flooding both Earth and sky.

According to *Arizona Highways Magazine*, appreciation of the Grand Canyon is universal. Recently, it was named as a World Cultural and Natural Heritage Site, one of 112 sites selected for this recognition by the United Nations Educational, Scientific, and Cultural Organization. The Canyon has exerted its sweeping influence on explorers and adventurers, writers and philosophers, scientists and laymen of all nations and races. Its effect on their senses and sensibilities has resulted in some the most evocative passages ever penned about the natural environment and the place of humankind in it. For its beauty, its scale, its inspirational and emotional impact, it surely qualifies as Temple of The World.

This description certainly helps us to understand the state motto more fully: *Ditat Deus*, "God Enriches."

"Doggie"

I had been flying in Arizona a while when I attended a pancake feed fly-in in Show Low. They had griddles and tables set up in one of the large hangers. I noticed a World War I 1917 German Albatross D.V., an authentic looking biplane fighter including a machine gun mounted on the top wing. Soon I saw a rustic looking pilot outfitted in a weathered leather jacket with a few interesting, colorful patches on it. He must be the pilot of the open cockpit vintage machine. The gentleman with the grizzled face and overstated white handlebar mustache was already sitting down with his plate and agreed that I could join him. The conversation was easy and before I left, asked Doggie what his secret was. He said, "Just keep move'n." The brevity of his explanation was not wasted on me. I only regret that I did not take the time to visit him on his home field of Rimrock, the oldest, longest continually functioning airfield in Arizona. Forest "Doggie" Kline passed away from a stroke on October 27, 2004. He was 83 years young and flew on his terms right up till the very end. He was, what I call, a Master Pilot.

Over a 14-year period, I flew the Skyhawk between Phoenix and Central City, Nebraska, dozens of times. I knew the route well and always planned a fuel stop in Pueblo, Colorado, on the way out and Alamosa, Colorado, on the return flight. Both were near the midway point of the eight-hour trip. My preferred altitude for the normally aspirated engine was 10,500 feet, depending on the outside air temperature and winds aloft. That altitude was near the service ceiling of the 172 during the extreme summertime heat. Sometimes flying low level over the Rocky Mountains, I would confront significant winds. On one trip to Nebraska with Joyce, east of Alamosa, we encountered an unyielding high-pressure system but steady northerly flow. Navigating around the lee aspect of the 14,344 foot (14er) Blanca Peak, to maintain my track across the ground, I had to initiate a 45 degree crab with the airplane. Joyce looked out the window and commented, "Are we going sideways?" Indeed, it's called crabbing, and it was quite dramatic. "Yes," I explained, "we were heading one way to go another." I was delighted that we were not getting pounded with vicious rotors or downdrafts from the massif.

A few years later, I was reminded of this scenario with Joyce when we landed in Central City, Nebraska, just ahead of a blizzard. That time, four of us were trying to push that same 172 into a hanger while the wind was skidding it sideways on the snow packed ramp. You had to be aggressively smart to deal with windy and potentially dangerous situations on the ground.

On return trips from Nebraska, I frequently flew north of Blanca Peak, wind permitting. As soon as I crossed the saddle on the north-south ridge, I found myself directly over the majestic Great Sand Dunes National Monument. They are the tallest dunes in North America and always appeared so well groomed and symmetric. But when taking the 172 from Phoenix to San Diego, we overflew an even more extensive area of dunes outside of Yuma Arizona, The Imperial Sand Dunes National Recreation Area. These dunes were classically beautiful, expansive, and I feel compelled somehow, to travel the extent of them one day on foot. They are one of the nation's largest central area of sand dunes and extend for more than 40 miles along the eastern edge of California's Imperial Valley.

While these sand dunes fit nicely into their arid surroundings, I had found a more surprising area of dunes in the Kobuk Valley of Alaska. They were the Great Kobuk Sand Dunes located in the Kobuk Valley National Park in the northwestern Arctic of Alaska. Three areas of dune fields are situated on the south side of the Kobuk River. The Great Kobuk Sand Dunes, Little Kobuk Sand Dunes, and the Hunt River Dunes are all remnants of the larger dune field that covered as many as 200,000 acres immediately after the retreat of the Pleistocene glaciation. I was always captivated by the dichotomy of sand dunes that looked so out of place. They seemed like an exclusive and natural playground in the expanse of the Arctic tundra.

Great Sand Dunes National Monument, Colorado.
Photographer Randy Lippincott.

Most of the flights from Nebraska back to Arizona in the 172 were low-level nap-of-the-earth due to predominant headwinds. The good news is that I saw a lot of the countryside up close and personal. The real hazards, of course, were radio towers and guy wires. You can only make that mistake once. A single tower can spoil your entire trip. It does add stress to the journey and demands that you pay constant attention to the surroundings. In addition to man-made obstacles, the terrain gradually gains elevation on the westbound leg, so my altitude frequently needed to be adjusted upward.

I made early morning departures on those summer trips to cross the Rocky Mountains before midday and the predictable formation of problematic severe thunderstorms. On one of those "bug smashing" excursions, I encountered some wonderfully vast sweeping fields of sunflowers in western Kansas. It was the grandest uniform expanse of sunflowers that I had ever witnessed. Since I was westbound with the early morning sun to my back, all of the sunflower heads were synchronized and turned eastward, directly facing me and the sun. Every single sunflower petal was bathed in the brilliant glow of the early morning dulcet sunlight. The magnificent rolling fields of endless gleaming yellow sunflowers, like nature's solar panels, filled my low-level vista. That glorious world class National Geographic photo is preserved in my mind. I didn't want the mesmerizing visual stimulation to end and will always recall it fondly.

Soon that vision collided with the destructive forces of the devastating varmint called prairie dog. Prairie dogs are prolific and dig up crops and pristine grassy pasturelands. From the air, this prairie dog town appeared as a ruinous scourge on the earth. The vermin's pocks are characteristic, widespread, and quite damaging to the land. You would be considered unlucky to have a prairie dog town located on your property. I remember that my father told me how they hunted the elusive rodents for long distance shooting sport when he was a kid.

On those Nebraska trips during the mid-1990s, I saw frequent massive summertime wildfires northeast of metropolitan Phoenix on my climb to cruising altitude. I typically departed at 3:00 a.m. for the eight-hour flight and flames would frequently silhouette the nighttime skyline. No matter how high I climbed in the 172, sooner or later, the characteristic smell of wildfire would sift through the cabin. The lightning-sparked 1995 Rio Fire blackened 36 square miles in the McDowell Mountains and surrounding area.

While touring Arizona, I discovered "The Boneyard." It is a striking and an unusual place, adjacent to Davis-Monthan Air Force Base in Tucson. It's called The Boneyard because that's where the Air Force parks all of its old airplanes. These are planes that the military is not ready to get rid of but are out of service and mothballed in a large area of the desert adjacent to the airbase. Before 9/11, I could fly down to Tucson and orbit the Boneyard at any reasonable altitude for as long as I wanted, just to sightsee. Following 9/11, it became restricted airspace; however, once again the Boneyard allows public viewing, and now it is even open to ground traffic tours. When the B-52Gs were withdrawn from service in the early 1990s, the last one was delivered to the salvage yard in Arizona on May 5, 1994. They were subsequently destroyed in compliance with the Strategic Arms Limitation Treaty (START) of 1991. Over time, I watched as the massive field of 365 of the faithful G-model giant bombers, all parked with interlocking wingtips, were systematically chopped up. Don't get me wrong; there are still plenty of all types of airplanes (thousands) to view. Having grown up with the Stratofortress, I found the scene to be the sad end of an era.

A Close Call and a Comet

It was dusk, and I was on my way down to Tucson for dinner, flying at 7,500 feet and had passed Marana Airpark, the CIA airport. I was already talking to Tucson approach and had been given a squawk and positive radar identification. Then, without warning, out of my 7 o'clock position, I was surprised by a Jumbo Boeing 747, seemingly climbing rapidly out from under my left wing. Nobody said anything until "Air America" asked to pick up his clearance, "present position direct, Bangor, Maine, out of one zero thousand." He had taken off from a non-towered airfield, was climbing out under VFR rules: and was picking up his IFR clearance about the same time I was picking myself up off of the floor. Holy shit! I hope he saw me. Well, it was too late to do anything, and I was parallel to his overwhelming wake turbulence! Although it was a bit close and intimidating, I marveled at the magnificent sight bathed in the last illuminating rays of light. I knew all my strobe lights were on, and I was sure the pilot was thinking the same thing that the cocky A-6 jet jockey at the Dalles thought that morning, "Now why don't I give him something to write home about, just as he ignited his afterburners!"

The trip home from Tucson that night in November of 1996 was routine but just as memorable as the first leg of the flight. My intentional best view of a comet was from 12,500 feet while flying back from Tucson. The Hale-Bopp comet was dubbed the Great Comet of 1997. It became visible to the human eye by May 1996 and stayed visible for an extended period. In the pitch dark well away from the big city lights, it was like I could reach out and touch it. The view was crystal clear and a fantastic sight of a rarely seen meteorological event. Wow, I had no idea that earlier a much more personal and up-close incident was going to preempt the heavenly phenomena.

A Bloody Anzio Landing

In November 1996 I had flown to Anzio Landing on Falcon Field in Mesa, which was my preferred venue for Italian food. Sometimes, on these dinner excursions, I would make a circle tour of the greater Phoenix area on the return trip; however, this time I headed straight back to Scottsdale where I kept my plane hangared. It was just after 9:00 p.m. and I noted that ATIS stated that the airfield was closed. What? That had to be a mistake. I needed to land there to park the airplane and pick up my car. Although the tower was scheduled to be closed, that didn't mean the airport was also closed. I called them for clarification, and they answered. There had been an unfortunate nighttime crash, and the runway was blocked. I had to divert to Deer Valley Airport and call someone for a ride that night and then pick up my car at Scottsdale.

The following was taken from the NTSB report generated about that night:

> Three Die in Scottsdale Airport Crash, November 21, 1996. A single-engine plane was coming in for a landing, crashed on the runway in Scottsdale, Arizona, lost control and veered into an empty corporate jet, killing all three onboard. The four-seat Mooney was attempting to land at the Scottsdale Airport around 8:20 p.m. Thursday when it crashed. Scottsdale Airport is the busiest single-runway facility in the country, according to the city's Chamber of Commerce.

It was a tragic event that is repeated at night more often than we care to admit. Nighttime ramifications are exponentially more dangerous than they are during daylight hours. Pilots need to be more proficient at night to be current, and the preflight planning needs to be much more detailed to complete a safe flight.

A headline-grabbing nighttime crash occurred on July 16, 1999, when John F. Kennedy Jr. crashed his Piper Saratoga. The loss of control happened because of the susceptible low time pilot (310 hours) in a "new model" high-performance aircraft at night in hazy conditions. He was attempting to fly into Martha's Vineyard, Massachusetts, in marginal weather conditions. The accident was the often-repeated mistake of spatial disorientation and subsequent loss of aircraft control when there was no outside horizon for reference. As these disasters show, nighttime landings and departures are riskier than the typical daytime flights. The airport facilities directory describes the prudent departure procedures for any particular runway for safe obstacle clearance in reduced visibility. But the pilot must still be proficient at flying without reference to the horizon.

During January 2003, I vividly recall a 1980 Piper Aerostar that departed Scottsdale for Santa Fe, New Mexico; he made a right turn out and flew into the McDowell Mountains in the dark. The pilot failed to follow the well-established departure procedures for terrain clearance. In November 2011, a Safford, Arizona, man flying a Rockwell AC69 twin-engine plane picked up his three children in Mesa. He was taking them back to Safford for the holiday weekend when he flew into the nearby Superstition Mountains on a moonless night. Declared pilot error by the NTSB, he failed to follow the departure procedures for obstacle clearance on that familiar runway. Both cases were nighttime CFIT; they never saw it coming.

Haboob

One evening after work in January of 1998, I was headed across town to dinner in the 172, like I had done so many times before. As soon as I departed Deer Valley, I turned south and contacted Phoenix Approach. No sooner had the words left my mouth, when I saw the full-blown and impressive Haboob (the Arabic word for desert sandstorm) approaching from the south. It was a wall of dirt over 2,000 feet high, 20 miles long, and rapidly advancing. Just like in the movies, it was ugly and awesome at the same time. There was no way I was flying into that! Without fanfare, I made an about face and returned to Deer Valley. I parked the airplane and got in the car. However, I was still headed into the same dirt storm, just in traffic on the freeway. I started to wonder why I would make the same mistake two times in a row. It was almost as bad as being on the airplane and there was no way to get out of it by climbing over the storm. Okay, so I'm a slow learner. In the car, someone could stop in front of you, or if you pulled over, you should plan on being rear-ended. It simply was not a good idea to be out in the severe low visibility situation. It was extremely hazardous in the air or the car.

Emergency Adventure

On another occasion, Kalvan Swanky and his brother Barron called me for the original "emergency adventure." We planned a last-minute weekend climbing and biking trip to Moab, Utah. I flew them in the Columbia 400 to Moab, Utah, where we rented a jeep. That day we rock climbed in beautiful Indian Creek. It was all sandstone splitter cracks; my favorite was "Super Crack." In a word, it was perfectly unrivaled. The second day we rented full suspension mountain bikes and rode them from town out to Slickrock. It was my first time on a mountain bike, and I was at the limits of my ability. The roundtrip from Moab on the bike (7.4 miles to the Slickrock trailhead plus 10.5 technical miles for the loop) challenged my endurance, and I was ready to return to Scottsdale. Thankfully, it was partly cloudy, and I was not completely dehydrated. Back at the Moab airport, we loaded the Columbia and headed home. I checked the weather, and the forecast was for blowing dirt up to 12,000 feet in the Four Corners region. Sure enough, we had to climb to 16,500 feet to get over it. At that altitude, the headwinds were 60 knots, and although we didn't see an organized Haboob, we could see the dirt-filled storm raging in the desert far below us.

Lac Vieux Desert

My favorite impromptu flying trip of all time was in the Grumman Goose with Bill and Myrt Rose. I met Bill through work, and while I was in Chicago, he invited me to stay at their house. We both had a passion for aviation and Bill shared his enthusiasm with me. Our first excursion was in his personal Bell Jet Ranger to the roof landing pad of the expansive Rose Meat Packing Company. At home, the helicopter rested on a 12 x 12-foot platform that was on rails used to roll it out of the hanger. After the door was open, a single push button positioned the Jet Ranger outdoors ready for departure. After our preflight, we made a beeline to the company roof helipad, and then the impressive VIP tour of the meatpacking facility. After that, we departed in the helicopter to the Mill Rose Restaurant for lunch. Wow, I could get used to this; it was true door-to-door service. Later that afternoon I was privileged to tour Bill's private aviation department and the Ryan Aircraft restoration shop at the Mill Rose Farm in Barrington, Illinois. (Yes, the same type of vintage aircraft that Harrison Ford crash-landed on a golf course in California near Santa Monica in March 2015.) I would have been happy to have spent all my time in that amazing machine shop.

I met Winston for the first time at the main Rose house and airfield. Winston was a beautifully restored blue and yellow Piper Cub that was Myrt Rose's pride and joy. It was the airplane that she learned to fly in and, which, years later Bill located and had completely restored. He surprised Myrt with it as a birthday gift, where she found the Cub at home on the Rose grass strip out behind the house. But much later, in August 2011, the *Deseret News* reported:

> Myrtle Rose was taking a short flight over suburban Chicago when the 75-year-old aviation enthusiast looked out her cockpit window to see two F-16 fighter jets. She assumed the military pilots were just slowing down to get a closer look at her antique plane.

Inadvertently Myrt had strayed into a temporarily restricted airspace due to a presidential visit. Ouch! To make it worse, she didn't even have her radio on, just minding her own business in the otherwise uncontrolled airspace. She still has her license but had to fill out a lot of paperwork. Myrt told me that the most embarrassing thing about the mishap was that they printed her age in the paper.

On this trip, I was to make one last departure on that aesthetically groomed runway. It was in the magnificently beautiful and vintage twin-engine Goose. The Grumman G-21 Goose is an amphibious aircraft that was designed to serve as an eight-seat "commuter" aircraft for businessmen in the Long Island area, circa 1937. The Goose was Grumman's first monoplane to fly, its first twin-engine aircraft, and its first aircraft to enter commercial airline service. During World War II, the Goose became an effective transport for the U.S. military (including the United States Coast Guard), as well as serving with many other air forces. During hostilities, the Goose took on an increasing number of combat and training roles.

We departed the grass strip to the north and leveled off under 3,000 feet. Our destination was Lac Vieux Desert (translated "Lake of the Old Clearing") in upper Wisconsin about 320 miles to the north of the Mill Rose Farm. It was not far south of Lake Superior and just east of Land O' Lakes. This forested area was God's country, and I was in for a treat. At our cruising altitude, however, it didn't seem that we were going all that fast across the ground. After looking around for any extra drag, I noticed that the gear was still extended. Retracting the landing gear improved our ground speed considerably!

As we approached the private island from the west end of the lake, we overflew the island and started our approach to landing into the wind as we turned to the southwest. Above all else, it was critical that the gear was retracted for a water landing. A wheels-down landing on water could cause the aircraft to flip over when it touched down. All I had to do was set the power, flaps, nail the approach airspeed, and let the airplane fly onto the water. Once we landed, the amphibious hull rapidly slowed us in the slightly choppy water. As we taxied in the lake to the eastern edge of the secluded, but a sizable island, Bill lowered the landing gear. I watched as experience took over; in a practiced move, he taxied the Goose out of the water and did an 180 degree turn on the sloping steel ramp (Marston Matting from World War II). It had been a perfect flight, and we deplaned a few yards from the front door of the house. What I failed to see when we flew over his island was the helipad and the Maule on amphibious floats, just west of the house where there was another private ramp. It was on this secluded island that I learned about Bill's affiliation with Al Capone, his run-in with the law, and his colorful youth.

The Bill Rose Grumman Goose at Lac Vieux Desert.
Photographer Randy Lippincott.

The Big Steep

I took up my old discipline of rock climbing in January 2001 when I wanted to become more physical again and went on a couple of Sierra Club outings. Soon I met Jim Sowden, and we began climbing together regularly. It wasn't long before we decided to try an alpine ascent of the 13,770-foot Grand Teton Mountain, which is one of the 50 Classic Climbs of North America. Routinely, we boulder during the week and climb local multi-pitch rock on the weekends. It was a long hot summer for us, and we looked forward to the crisp temperatures that Wyoming offered.

At 4:33 a.m. the tires lifted off the Deer Valley runway for Page, Arizona, on our way to Jackson Hole, Wyoming. A light tailwind, rocking-chair smooth ride, and a fresh flow of air from the vents made for a great start. At altitude, I trimmed the airplane, the stereo was cranking out "Graceland" by Paul Simon in our headsets, and I handed the controls to my co-pilot. I dimmed the cabin lights and settled into my seat with a sense that it wouldn't be long before we would see the first hint of orange over the horizon to the east.

It was a fabulous outing. My climbing partner Jim and I made the six-hour flight to Jackson Hole in two parts. First, we flew four hours to Salt Lake City where we stayed and climbed in Little Cottonwood Canyon—my old stomping ground, "The School Room." Unfortunately, Jim seriously sprained his ankle while bouldering on a warm-up, which hampered our practice climbing activities. We did enjoy a spending spree at REI and the Black Diamond store in Salt Lake City. While in Salt Lake, we slept at 9,500 feet. At the very top of Little Cottonwood Canyon, above Alta Ski Resort, we lounged for two days to help us acclimatize. It was a nice cool shakedown and lent itself to some short scenic hikes. I was unable to contact any old friends, but we had a great time sightseeing and breathing the mountain air.

My flight in the Cessna to Jackson Hole Wyoming was 1:50 minutes. Before landing, we photographed and checked out the nearly 14,000-foot peak from the 11,000-foot level of the east face. We live in the most beautiful country, and the mountains are breathtaking and more exalted each time I visit them. We picked up a rental car and headed to Star Valley Ranch where Sharon and Jim Chumley, my high school wrestling coach, were kind enough to let us bunk while they were in Alaska on a cruise. We read and lounged, which gave Jim's ankle a few more days to recover for the big event. On the satellite, we picked up *Mutiny on the Bounty* and *True Grit* for our evening entertainment.

Our approach to the upper saddle and campsite was long and uneventful. After we had decided on the traditional Exum route via Wall Street, we donned our climbing shoes, harnesses, and roped up on Wall Street. I started out with the hand traverse at the exposed gap, pausing long enough to gaze down between my legs into the abyss. The rock was in perfect shape, and the remainder of the climb was spectacular. Near the last technical pitch close to the summit, something caught my eye. As I extended my neck, I focused on a beautifully sleek, all white sailplane. The pilot was using air currents off the face of the Grand Teton for lift. Somewhat of a technologic dichotomy; he was close to 14,000 feet and glided right over my head without effort or sound. It helped me realize that tools aided our progress on the rock just as his path through the air was made possible by a non-motorized machine. His hands on synthetic controls, as my fingers caressed the natural stone. His tennis shoes applied pressure to the rudder pedals, as my tightly bound feet danced on tiny granite footholds.

> As a kid, I knew two things to be self-evident.
> Flying: Believe it, and it'll happen.
> Superpowers: Bound to be something—spinach or
> whatever will do the trick. Climbing is my flying and
> coffee is my spinach.
> —Peter Croft

We arrived at the upper snowfields and the summit at 2:00 p.m. Our visibility was unrestricted, and nearly 100 miles away we could easily see the forest fires in Yellowstone. The volcanic looking smoke was being pumped upwards to 20,000 feet; well above our vantage point. We took pictures, visited with some other climbers on the mountain and marveled at the outstanding panorama. I remembered other peaks I had visited in all sorts of weather. This summit had to rank as one of the best.

> Mountains are fantastic examples of the power and
> mystery of nature, and the routes we climb on them
> are expressions of all that is best in the human spirit.
> —Michael Kennedy

The descent had a thrilling 120-foot free rappel, and it was nearly 5:00 p.m. when we reached our little yellow tent. It wasn't long before we were horizontal and started the rehydration process with cocoa, the main course of black beans and rice, and then a sweet blueberry cobbler!

Even climbers and pilots are subject to basic needs. We were privy to the privy at 11,300-feet; it's a two-holer, for those old enough not to need an explanation. The out-of-doors facility sat on the west side of a sizable boulder open to earth and heavens. Apparently, it had been designed as open-air to facilitate servicing it with a helicopter. As you sat on the throne, your view to the west was spectacular and unimpaired. I faithfully watched the sun go down from that inviting seat. If you were not concerned about your exposure, the vista tended to protract the event.

During our descent, we were approached by a couple on the trail who asked us for a ride to the highway, which we were obliged to accommodate. By the time we looked for the pair in the parking lot, they were nowhere to be found. Later at The Pizza and Pasta in Moose Junction, we learned they had caught a ride with a five-time astronaut. Damn! Stood up for an astronaut; I wish I had a nickel for every time I heard that excuse.

Unfortunately, the trek took its toll on our poorly conditioned legs, and we didn't feel the need for any additional climbs or even the effort of local fly fishing. We checked in at the American Alpine Club Climbers Ranch for $6/night and headed out for pasta and cold beer. From our seat in the restaurant, we watched thunderclouds roll in and lightning pick at the majestic peak. The timing of our lofty adventure had been impeccable. We packed and reluctantly headed for the airport the following day. After waiting our turn between jets, we departed and headed south up the wild and scenic Greys River. Our route went past the sleepy village of Heber along the eastern border of the Wasatch and through Provo Canyon. We stopped in old and familiar Richfield, Utah, for fuel to ensure against any unplanned off airport landing.

Reaching the Grand Canyon, we had to deviate around scattered thundershowers. The eastern portion of the canyon was smoke filled. As we approached, we noticed the fire generating the dynamically fluid white cloud was south of the canyon, and the wind was from the south. Apparently, the heavier cold air was keeping it on the ground and pushing the pure white smoke down into the canyon. From our vantage point, the billowing smoke looked like Niagara Falls pouring into the insatiable abyss. A setup for the definitive Ed Mell painting, the afternoon light, smoke, and dominant thunderstorm in the background was a spectacular sight to behold. Our six and a half hour flight home was straight forward until crossing into Arizona. We were forced to divert seventy miles west of Prescott just to avoid a band of dangerous thunderstorms north of Phoenix. In Scottsdale, we were greeted by gusting wind and blowing dirt.

> Limitations live only in our minds. But if we use our imaginations, our possibilities become limitless.
> —Jamie Paolinetti

Weeks later at Falcon Field, it was time for some regular maintenance. I had always changed the oil in the 172 and over time had become proficient at it. Although I don't recall being in a big hurry, I had the disposal bucket that I drained the used oil into in place. It always took awhile to empty the sump completely. While waiting, I would set up the funnel, loosen the oil caps, and line up the eight black quart containers of fresh oil. However, I must have been in the zone listening to some Pink Floyd…so dutifully, I started the ritual task of dumping oil directly into the funnel. You guessed it, just before emptying the last quart, I noticed that I had not closed the drain valve. Oops! The new oil had been running straight through the engine and into the waste container. The first thing that I did was to ensure that the pea-brained act had not been witnessed by anyone nearby.

Monument Valley, Red Bull Airstrip

Joyce Berk (my then girlfriend and later my wife) first flew with me in the Skyhawk to scenic Monument Valley in May 2004. She met me at my house at 5:00 a.m. for the pleasant very early start to circumnavigate one-third of the state of Arizona in my white and black 172. The takeoff was smooth, and it wasn't long after we reached cruising altitude that I detected the first rays of pink pastel sunlight brushing the eastern horizon.

Not far northeast of Phoenix, we crossed the Mogollon Rim, an escarpment, about 2,000 feet high, extending diagonally from central Arizona to Southwest New Mexico. In part, it separates the Colorado Plateau from the Basin and Range region to the south. The Rim country contains the largest continuous forest of Ponderosa Pine in the world.

Further on, I made a beeline to the historical Meteor Crater, which was impressive and nicely contrasted in the shadows of the early morning light. I had photographed the 50,000-year-old nearby Meteor Crater during my first excursion to Arizona in 1976. The nearly perfect solitary defect on the otherwise barren desert is about halfway between Flagstaff and Winslow, Arizona; it is visible at great distances from the air. I remember how excited I was to see it for the first time. As uniquely impressive, it was created in mere nanoseconds, compared to the millions of years taken by the Colorado River to carve away the gorge of the Grand Canyon. The Barringer Meteor Crater is an impressive and extraordinary impact crater, 3,900 feet wide and 560 deep. Its formation displaced 160 million tons of rock in a fraction of a second, and the energy was equivalent to a ten megaton nuclear bomb. In later years, I visited the site and learned about the B612 project whose critical mission is to find asteroids or near-Earth objects (NEO) before they find us.

I love the diverse expanses of the Intermountain West, from Baja to Barrow, and have toured most of it by air. I will never grow weary of these natural wonders.

After our pass over Meteor Crater, we continued north, and the landscape became a shrub-dotted barren region. Further north, it became grasslands that later merged into woodlands of oak and chaparral. In the high temperate areas, we discovered forests of Piñon Pine and Juniper trees. Familiar to this region are the black bear, mountain lion, desert bighorn sheep, whitetail and mule deer, antelope, and elk.

The Barringer Meteor Crater in Northern Arizona.
Photographer Randy Lippincott.

Next, it was onto the expansive open pit coal mines of the Navajo Nation. The Navajo Kayenta Mine on the amazing Black Mesa in northern Arizona is just south of Monument Valley and is both surprising and impressive. It is the largest coal deposit in the United States. This immense strip mining area on the Navajo Indian Reservation supplies coal to the power plant in Page, Arizona. From miles away, we spotted the three giant 14-story-tall electric draglines that each weigh 9.8 million pounds, support a 300-foot boom, and operate a bucket that removes 200 tons of material in a single bite. From there, the coal was loaded onto trucks where it is taken to a central location, crushed, and placed on a conveyer belt 17 miles in length! It is an easy landmark to spot from the air due to the prominent three dragline type behemoths. At the other end of the conveyor, it is loaded on a dedicated train and hauled 80 miles to the Navajo Generation Station. Nearby, an experimental 18-inch pipeline transported a coal-slurry 275 miles west to the Mohave Generating Station in Bullhead City on the Colorado River. For over 30 years, the Peabody Coal Company pumped a billion gallons of water per year from the Black Mesa aquifer, the sole water source for the Hopi and Navajo peoples of the region. The pipeline was closed, and the Mohave Generating Station was dismantled in 2005.

I started my descent over the village of Kayenta and entered majestic Monument Valley. During my aerial tour, I tried to point out and name the well-known landmarks. My favorite is the Totem, primarily because of its climbing connection to the movie, *The Eiger Sanction,* starring Clint Eastwood. We were in the barren desert; it was not a populated area and maybe I went lower than the top of the Totem to give Joyce an up close look at it. We flew around a bit and landed on the small strip at Goulding's Trading Post. We had breakfast there, took in the sights, and pondered the local history in the free museum.

The modern-day history of Monument Valley started with Harry and Mike Goulding in 1939. Goulding's Trading Post is a lodge, a trading post, and a museum located just north of the Arizona-Utah border, adjacent to the Navajo Tribal Park in Monument Valley. Harry Goulding introduced director John Ford to the remote Monument Valley where he shot several of his ageless westerns. The 1939 movie *Stagecoach* created three icons: John Wayne, John Ford, and the 30,000 acres of red sandstone glory on the Utah-Arizona border known as Monument Valley. It was a pioneering rancher, Harry Goulding, who brought Hollywood to his Navajo home, and helped shape America's vision of the "Wild West."

The remote runway at Gouldings was paved in 2007, explicitly for the Red Bull air races. Subsequently, it was possible for me to land with the Columbia 400 on the hard surface. Otherwise, the small tires would unacceptably sink into the loose sand. I had personally witnessed a Piper 140 flip up onto its nose when attempting to land on the marginal strip. Slightly off-center, the right wheel caught the loose sand on the edge of the runway and uncontrollably forced it into the ditch and an untimely dilemma.

The Totem, seen in the rock climbing movie, *The Eiger Sanction*
with Clint Eastwood. Photographer Randy Lippincott.

After departure, we headed over to the arid confluence of the San Juan and Colorado Rivers. From there I flew low-level "down river" to Rainbow Bridge, the world's largest natural stone bridge. I monitored the "up river" flight-seeing traffic frequency while we circled the natural wonder. Next, it was on to more wild and scenic beautiful Lake Powell. Formidable views unfolded around every corner of the dazzling red sandstone cliffs and expanse of placid blue water. The lake beaches and rocky escarpments are bifurcating and extensive with more scenic shoreline (1,960 miles) to cruise than the West Coast of the United States. Every beach, every cove, and every tributary were more resplendent than the former. Even today, each time I visit Lake Powell, I always ask myself, "Why has it been so long since my last visit to this rugged and breathtaking paradox in the desert?"

The hydroelectric Glen Canyon Dam is near Page, Arizona, where we made our next stop to freshen up and ponder the scenic views. We flew downriver over Lee's Ferry and the upper reaches of the Grand Canyon. Then we turned south toward the 12,637-foot summit of Humphrey's Peak. Since my days of flying for skydivers, I appreciate flying very close to imposing rocky faces. But before I do, I always carefully assess the wind flow and local conditions. An up-close approach to Humphrey's Peak can be formidable. That day, I was rewarded with spotting hikers on the summit in the calm conditions. I didn't know it then, but I would later use the same aircraft that I had used to spread Marti's father's ashes over the Columbia Glacier to discharge remains over the San Francisco Peaks. It was a fellow orthopedist, Bob Johnson M.D., a hardcore skier whom I would "take home" to his beloved ski slopes.

Before Joyce and I started our descent over Sedona, I wanted to finesse her with some negative Gs. As she opened her tin of Altoids, I asked if she wanted to see them float. They all went up in the air, and all but one made it back into its container—and it took place without making Joyce sick. I think that was the moment that I started to fall for her. We had circumnavigated a third of Arizona and had seen the state's finest attractions. By the time we were back in Scottsdale, it had been an eight hour day. Joyce had done it all without a single complaint! She was quietly earning my copilot's seat.

In the Arizona desert, we sleep with the windows open most of the winter while the weather is pleasant. When we were first married, Joyce told me that in the early morning hours while she was unable to sleep, and I was sleeping soundly, she noticed that my breathing would suddenly go silent, as if to listen intently when an airplane flew overhead. Joyce said the reaction was predictable, repeatable, and uncanny. It seemed that I was taking a mandatory survey and had to identify and log each aircraft that flew within my hearing range during the hours of dawn. Yes, even while asleep I was still a pilot. Joyce noted that I would momentarily cease my heavy breathing as I strained to hear and let the aviator in me take over.

N6897N

I had an opportunity to join a loose flying partnership in a Cessna 210. The group had a principal owner and three or four members who paid hourly rates. In November of 2004, Mike Feliksa and I flew commercially to Detroit, Michigan, to pick up the 1979 T210, N6897N in nearby Pontiac. I was tasked with the duty because I was the only one in the group who was insurable; that is, I had prior experience in that model of the fast airplane. The sign-off for my original turbo 210 checkout had been December 13, 1976, in Provo, Utah.

When we arrived in Pontiac, I inspected the airplane; the run-up was good, and I reviewed all the paperwork. In no time, we were airborne and headed back to Phoenix in a great airplane. Unable to cross the Rocky Mountains due to weather and no onboard oxygen, we ended up staying overnight with my parents in Central City, Nebraska. We had a good "partnership" on the airplane, and everyone had different needs and time constraints for the six-place aircraft. I loved that T210, and we had an excellent arrangement. We parked N6897N in Hangar #13 at the beautiful, but small Carefree gated private airport. It was as close to my house as any airport had ever been. I was enjoying the arrangement and felt no urgency in selling my own economic 172 that came with me from Alaska.

Cousin Karin and David Stern flew in the T210 with us to Death Valley and later to Cedar City, Utah, for a visit. For some reason, the trim in combination with the weight and balance was terribly askew. When I tried to start our descent, even with the power reduced, I had to forcefully use both arms with locked elbows on the yoke to push and hold the nose down. It was manageable, but very disconcerting and clearly not normal. I was thinking back to the moose hunters who lost control of the Cessna 185 outside of Fairbanks in November 1987. I didn't want to lose command of the aircraft if the nose would suddenly pitch up. It could end in a tragedy, not unlike so many others had done.

I was happy that I kept my personal 172, and the partnership on the T210 worked nicely until March 22, 2005. Mike had five large men with him when he returned from a day trip to eastern Arizona. He made an overhead approach from the east, descended to pattern altitude, and on his final leg with flaps and gear extended, saw that he was low. Immediately, Mike bumped the throttle, but because the boost pump was turned on, it automatically switched to high boost and flooded the engine. He crash-landed short of runway 24 at Carefree. Fortunately, there was no fire. We only had possession of the T210 for a total of five months.

As soon as Mike was out of the airplane and made certain that everyone was safe, he called me. I told him that he was in shock and NOT to make any statement to the authorities. I instructed him that his next phone call should immediately be to the AOPA Legal Counsel. They would advise him what to do and debrief him every step of the way. It was a traumatic event for all involved. Out of the six passengers, there was, unfortunately, one serious physical injury. Later, to demonstrate competency, Mike took a checkride with the FAA to get his license reinstated. He has flown with me in the ensuing years, but for all intents and purposes that was his last flight as pilot-in-command.

Official NTSB Report on the T210 Crash Landing

> The airplane hit the ground short of the runway following a failure of the engine to respond to throttle command on short final approach. The pilot said that on short final with the landing gear down and full flaps, the airplane started settling. The pilot added power and the engine failed to respond. The pilot said that it was his *habit to use the low fuel boost pump for landing* even though the *Pilot Owner Handbook* (POH) did not call for it. In the POH section 7, Airplane and System Descriptions, it shares an information note: "If the engine-driven fuel pump is functioning and the auxiliary fuel pump switch is placed in the ON position, an excessively rich fuel/air ratio is produced unless the mixture is leaned."

With the low (yellow) boost pump switch on during a reduced power approach, if the throttle is increased the boost pump goes to high and the engine can be flooded with an excessive rich mixture. According to the Cessna Pilot Safety and Warning Supplements booklet under Fuel Pressure Switch Operation/ Normal Auxiliary Fuel Pump Operation, it states in part: "During cruise, the auxiliary fuel pump(s) may be used at any time to clear excessive fuel vapor, as evidenced by an unstable fuel flow indication; however; the auxiliary fuel pump(s) should be turned off prior to descent. Failure to turn off the pump(s) could cause a power failure at reduced throttle settings or with a rapid throttle advance due to an excessively rich mixture, especially if the throttle switch rigging or fuel pressure switch settings are out of tolerance." No anomalies were found during an examination that would have precluded the engine from functioning normally.

Shortly after the incident with the 210, while we were out hiking, Joyce and I met a gentleman in Telluride, Colorado, who piloted a privately owned Boeing 757. Because we happened to be sitting on a huge boulder below a waterfall together having lunch, a polite conversation revealed our connection. As it turned out, he worked with the principle owner of our T210, N6897N. Joyce and I had previously made plans to fly the Centurion to Alaska that summer, and he knew all about it. Small world. On that July 4th weekend, we flew out of the high altitude Telluride airport in the normally aspirated Skyhawk, because the T210 had been unsalvageable. It was a disappointment to me that the runway didn't open until 7 a.m. I needed all of those oxygen molecules to be as close together as possible to generate the lift to depart safely from the highest commercial field in North America.

Hot and Windy

Devils Tower was my destination July 14, 2005. My regular climbing partner, Kalvan Swanky, and I scheduled time off, put together a climbing gear list, and consulted the guidebook for Devil's Tower in northeastern Wyoming. I was excited to attempt the clean, but an impossible looking collection of sheer vertical pentagonal columns. It was hot in Arizona, but with only two of us in the Cessna 172, and gear for our mission, weight was not an issue. We had visions of cold air and fair skies in the high chaparral of northern Wyoming. Kalvan met me at the airport, and we were off well before daylight. If Kalvan's brother Baron had been with us, he would have pronounced it, another "emergency adventure!" How could you argue with that rationale?

As we reached cruising altitude and fresh air, the airplane wanted to fly itself. We winged toward my favorite, Monument Valley, and past Grand Junction, Colorado. Along the west slope, we made good time against light headwinds and decided to stretch our legs and take on gas in Meeker, Colorado. It turned out to be a quaint village with a scenic sloping runway. We refueled, had a bite to eat, and taxied out to take off in the opposite direction that we had landed. When a field is not level, the general rule is land up-slope and takeoff downhill. We had a great start to this far-off striking destination for a climb. There was only one negative. In-flight service had been less than desirable on the first leg. I was hoping for it to improve on the next portion of our trip. However, instead, Kalvan had a very restful nap...leaving the "driving to me."

All along the west slope, we overflew manmade scars on the landscape, indicating gas and oil wells in an otherwise remote unpopulated mountainous countryside. As we headed north into Wyoming, we were met with headwinds—consistent headwinds—consistent strong headwinds that buffeted the small aircraft with heated plumes of parched air. To get "under the wind," I flew nap-of-the-earth across endless dry oceans of swaying prairie grass and tumbleweeds, ever vigilant for the occasional untimely cell tower; we weren't looking for THAT kind of reception. The harsh blistering wind and incessant turbulence made for a slow, tedious flight. There comes a time when you think, "Should I have driven?" The miles and hours dragged on. I glared at the GPS; it seemed like the numbers indicating the distance to our destination were increasing instead of decreasing—damn that digital device! I felt this was akin to what the settlers experienced in their prairie schooners on the way west, inching across this same endless dry virgin land. At last the control tower in Gillette, Wyoming, answered our call with permission to land. We were welcomed by the Fixed Base Operator (FBO) and taxied to a convenient transient parking space. Facing into the wind, we tied down the 172 before it was blown over. In due time, we unloaded the voluminous gear and secured our rental car. Now with air-conditioning, we headed to the village of Sundance, about 62 miles east for a sit-down meal and some well-earned rest.

After breakfast, we proceeded posthaste directly to Devils Tower. My first views were remarkable in the morning light. It was a colossal monolithic plug, projecting vertically from the surrounding rolling grassy plain—just like in *Close Encounters of the Third Kind*. One could easily imagine the parallel grooves in the rock to be bear claw marks as described in the following Indian legend:

> According to the Native American tribes of the Kiowa and Lakota Sioux, some girls went out to play and were spotted by several giant bears that began to chase them. To escape the bears, the girls climbed atop a rock, fell to their knees, and prayed to the Great Spirit to save them. Hearing their prayers, the Great Spirit made the rock rise from the ground towards the heavens so that the bears could not reach the girls. To climb the rock, the bears left deep claw marks on the sides, which had become too steep to climb. (Those are the marks which appear today on the sides of Devils Tower.) When the girls reached the sky, they were turned into the constellation Pleiades.

A more scientific account of the formation of Devils Tower states that about 65 million years ago during the Paleocene Period, the Rocky Mountains and the Black Hills were uplifted, but the process was compromised by a solitary plug of extruded magma. The rock mass cooled into the pentagonal and frequently hexagonal igneous upright columns that characterize this distinctively massive landmark. As cooling continued, these similarly formed massive parallel columns contracted to create vertical cracks between them, ideal for serious rock climbing. Devils Tower was our nation's first National Monument, proudly proclaimed by President Theodore Roosevelt in 1906 under the Antiquities Act. It was the same year that Roald Amundsen completed the first successful voyage through the Northwest Passage.

We registered with the Park Ranger for El Matador and were soon in the throes of climbing heaven. The second section of El Matador was the classic, definitive box stem ad infinitum.... Although rated difficult, it is far easier if you have longer legs than mine. A climber is held securely in place by pressing an outstretched foot against opposing columns, vis-à-vis the splits; your pelvis and gravity do the rest. Rope management can be facilitated almost anywhere in the uniform crack on the left side of the chute. There were good hand jams and finger locks, but sustained agonized stemming was the key to resting at any point. When I carefully executed this maneuver, I could only manage painful inches at a time. I was at my absolute limits. There is simply no way to "think" your legs longer than they are. This powerful waddle motion was akin to watching an inchworm on greased glass; with considerable effort, I was going nowhere fast.

> For me, an adventure is something that I can take an
> active part in but that I don't have total control over.
> —Peter Croft

The last part of the climb was not as severe or sustained. However, the upper section was exposed, and I began to feel vulnerable. The rock was "airy" well up on the west face, with a matching view. I wondered what those Indian maidens in the legend were thinking. After summit photos, we headed to the rappel station. We did meet other climbers on top but weren't prepared to hang around due to the lack of shade in the extreme heat. The scorching hot and unforgiving landscape redefined the word "Sundance." It had been a real sense of achievement in a remote setting and a spectacular rock formation. A mystical feeling came over me as I envisioned the long and varied history of this one-of-a-kind monument.

The following morning at a reasonable hour, and after another dose of Advil, we set off for Gillette, Wyoming, and the waiting 172. I had contacted my dear friend Senator Bill Hawks in Casper, Wyoming, and he agreed to host us for the night. Again, we flew nap-of-the-earth across Wyoming in the bumpy 172, all the while crabbing sideways during the flight to Casper in the stiff crosswind. Now, how could we have headwinds in both directions? Bill and Jan met us at the airfield in their Suburban. They graciously took us to their ranch house for a shower and change of clothes. After the white tablecloth steak dinner, there were stories and drinks until the wee hours. No one is more considerate and makes you feel more comfortable in conversation and their home than the senator and his hospitable wife.

Overstuffed beds, down comforters, and crisp sheets made us feel special and guaranteed a great night's rest. After breakfast, Kalvan and I were off to the airport and winging our way home in fair skies. We had some change in scenery on the return trip and made a point of flying over Monument Valley. I love to pick out all the monuments that I can name. It was a long flight through the Four Corners region, but I never tire of it. Again, more midday thermals and a taxing hot wind prolonged our journey. We made it to Winslow, Arizona, for fuel and to stretch our legs. From there on it was our "backyard." We overflew Jack's Canyon where I have made many weekend climbing outings. Near Payson, we saw angry columns of white smoke whipped by the uplifted scalding air. The water in natural vegetation consumed by the fire evaporates and forms steam. In turn, this colors the smoke white, and the rising air potentiates the wildfire drawing in fresh air to fuel the flames. Back at the Deer Valley Airport, I parked the Cessna, and we each headed to our respective homes. It had been a great trip, and I felt like I had pushed my vertical limits.

Columbia 400 G1000

In 2006, I took a formal class for the advanced navigation system. Then I was checked out in a G1000 equipped rental Cessna 172. After I was comfortable in the Skyhawk, I rented a G1000 equipped turbo 182. Joyce and I made a long cross-country flight to Cedar Rapids, Iowa, in the new airplane to my niece's wedding. The following spring, we acquired the Columbia 400 N2515Q, which was one of the first off the assembly line with the upgraded avionics in 2006. I still needed the practice to be comfortable with both flying the aircraft and utilizing the sophisticated instrumentation. A factory certified flight instructor was required for a check out to qualify for the aviation insurance. I also had a DVD computer based program to practice instrument approaches.

With time, the glass-cockpit has become second nature to me. A "glass-cockpit" is an indication that the instrument panel has, at least, two display screens: a primary function display (PFD) for the pilot and a multifunction display (MFD) for various presentations. That first summer I flew the Columbia 400 to the factory in Bend, Oregon. I took the nickel tour, went through the didactic training, and rigorous company flight check. It was well worth the time and I fell in love with the machine.

The integrated cockpit is considerably different from the old traditional style instrument panel with all of the "steam gauges." I remember overhearing a conversation my dad had with my brother when he started with Delta Air Lines. Loren was describing the cockpit on the Boeing 757 and the monitors in the instrument panel. He used the term "glass cockpit," and my Father lit up and his reply was, "Man, I bet that's quite a view from up there!" I guess he was assuming windows like the Plexiglas nose of the World War II B-24 and not the glass screens in the instrument panel that were monitors displaying the aircraft and flight information.

My fastest time from Deer Valley (DVT) to Central City (07K), which is a little under 900 nm was three hours and nine minutes. That was at 25,000 feet (and a little help from the jet stream) in the Columbia 400. Commonly, I plan to cruise at 200 knots (230 mph) when I cruise between 15-25,000 feet for long cross-country flights. It has been fun to fly the Columbia 400, and I love the G1000. Most likely when I sell the Columbia, I will be flying the yellow Super-Cub with tundra tires, very close to the ground just like my dad.

Aeronca Champ

In June 2012, I had an opportunity to ferry an Aeronca Champ back to Nebraska from Deer Valley. I retired from the medical field, so the time was my own. The little fabric covered aircraft had recently been restored by a good friend and was airworthy enough. I had flown a tail dragger when first learning in 1966 and understood the basics on a grass field. It was during the summer heat, and I was concerned that the underpowered engine might not have enough power to climb over the Rocky Mountains during daylight hours. I wanted to get a feel for the small aircraft and make some touch and goes before committing.

Since the airplane did not have a starter, I had to "hand prop" the engine to start it. Now hand propping a small engine is not difficult, but you do need to pay attention. The trick is to have the aircraft secured (read that, tied down) before starting. It is mandatory to have the throttle retarded to avoid an unintentional non-piloted taxi or uncontrolled takeoff. Once all the safety measures were in place, I practiced starting it until I became proficient. It didn't take long.

Next, it was time for some practice taxi maneuvers. As it turned out, I could only make right-hand turns, because the left brake was ineffective. I gave it some maintenance, and when I was finally satisfied, I called ground control and headed out to the runway. The takeoff and performance were uneventful. It was just like old times. After accelerating on the runway, I pushed the wheel forward to raise the tail off the ground, accelerated, and then held slight back pressure on the yolk to complete the very soft takeoff. Now, even in the pattern, the little airplane seemed underpowered, and doubt crept into my mind. Maybe it would not make it to the 10,000-foot level needed to cross the Rockies in the summertime heat.

The approach to landing appeared to be on a normal glideslope, and I was never apprehensive about landing the slow old bird. The airspeed and altitude looked good; everything was under control. I pulled the throttle back to let it settle down onto the long runway once I had the landing assured. At first contact with the blacktop, the little airplane acted like a spring. Unfortunately, my reaction when the main gear touched down was to pull slightly back on the control column. In conjunction with the bungee shock absorbers, even that small input initiated a "porpoise" action with the airplane. Quickly, I responded with the throttle, and instead of simply going around, (something that was a far off concept for me) I tried to continue with the landing. That was a mistake! Now, with all three wheels on the blacktop, somehow the right brake grabbed and instantly I was sideways on the runway. The airplane made an unexpected 60 degree turn to the right, and I was in real trouble!

My mind was clear, but my face went flush with absolute fear. At that moment, I knew a terrible accident was about to unfold in front of me, and unavoidably I was going to be the first to witness it. At that point, I felt like I was simply an observer. I would probably end up in a fireball alongside the runway. Thankfully, I took action and was able to save the little airplane and my skin. Immediately, I jammed the throttle to the firewall to get back up in the air. I was headed entirely in the wrong direction—sideways! I could visualize the airplane flipping over on the runway, collapsing the main landing gear; it would have been a catastrophic ground loop. I had no idea how I had just avoided a real catastrophe. It was as if I willed the airplane back into the sky in slow motion.

I was more thoughtful on the next landing, and it was uneventful—I never said perfect. I didn't even want to think about touching the right brake. When safely back in the hangar, I understood that I was not going to make the ferry flight back to the Midwest. I was euphoric to have avoided the self-induced near accident. I was also thankful that I did not bend the newly refurbished airplane. I was served a generous portion of humble pie...and I was not looking for seconds. The low-level aerobatic display had undoubtedly amused the tower operator.

The Last Word

A High-Speed Fly By….

And so it started with a dream, and it ends with a dream. Yes, 50 years do fly by, and one would hardly notice. I was so busy with life that time slipped away and the next thing I knew, it had been a half-century. It has been work. It has been fun. It has been a utility or means of all sorts of activities and pleasures for me. Today, the extended family has been well served and incredibly lucky to see the full gamut of aviation related pursuits: from military jets, airliners, piston aircraft, to fun general aviation, amphibious aircraft, flying on skis and floats, to the dangerous and trying commercial flying in the harsh Alaskan environment. I am grateful to have been there and to have sat in the front seat to the "Greatest Show on Earth."

To this day, I have safely flown all types of aircraft for more than 50 years. A half century seems like a long time to me…heck, it's most of my life. In 2016, I was awarded the coveted Wright Brothers Master Pilot Award (MPA) for my "dedicated service, technical expertise, professionalism, and outstanding contributions to further the cause of aviation." It was also in "recognition of my contributions to building and maintaining the safest aviation system in the world, through practicing and promoting safe aircraft flight operations for 50 consecutive years." It has been a long wild ride, and I am thankful to have safely made the odyssey.

My small rural community in central-eastern Nebraska has produced an incredible three Master Pilots: the first was Johnny Hruban, from Central City, and he was the flight instructor for both Daniel E. Tyler and me. We became Master Pilot Award recipients within months of each other in 2016. Each journey started on the little grass airfield at Central City. Johnny is retired from flight instruction, but Dan still flies LifeFlight helicopters full time in Australia. He served his country flying helicopters during the war in Vietnam, where he was decorated with the Distinguished Flying Cross, Bronze Star Medal X 2, Air Medal X 40, Purple Heart, and the Army Commendation Medal.

Most of my aviation career has been exhilarating yet uneventful. June 14, 2016, was the 50th anniversary of my first solo flight and was the presentation of the prestigious FAA Wright Brothers Master Pilot Award. It was a joyous event that was shared with many other aviators and lifelong friends of the family and my mother, Rosalie. Below is the FAA criteria for the coveted Wright Brothers Master Pilot Award. As a total surprise following that presentation, I was also awarded an honorary rank of Admiral in The Great Navy of the State of Nebraska. No one could ask for more than becoming Master and Commander in a single day.

Wright Brothers Master Pilot Award.
Photographer Randy Lippincott.

Wright Brothers Master Pilot Award

Eligibility

A. To be eligible for the Wright Brothers MPA, candidates must:
1) Have 50 years of U.S. piloting experience. The effective start date for the award is the date of the applicant's first solo flight or military equivalent.
2) Have held a FAA pilot certificate with 50 or more years of civil flying experience.
3) Have been a U.S. citizen, or permanent resident, during the 50 years of U.S. piloting experience.
B. Revocation of any airman certificate will disqualify a nominee for this award.
C. Prior accident history will be reviewed and considered on a case-by-case basis.
D. Prior enforcement actions (excluding revocation) are not necessarily disqualifying but will be reviewed on a case-by-case basis.

Aircraft I Have Flown

Some of my flight time has been in the following aircraft:

Aeronca Chief
BE 76 Duchess
BE 99 Airliner
Bell UH-1H Huey
Boeing 757 Full Motion Simulator
Cessna 120
Cessna 140
Cessna 150
Cessna 152
Cessna 170
Cessna 172 Skyhawk
Cessna 175 Skylark

Cessna 177 Cardinal

Cessna 182 Skylane

Cessna 182TRG

Cessna 205 Skywagon

Cessna 206 Super Skywagon

Cessna 207 Stationair

Cessna 208 Caravan

Cessna T210 Centurion

Cessna 441 Conquest

Cessna Citabria

Columbia 400

Diamond DV20 Katana

Evolution EVOT 550

General Dynamics F-16 Fighting Falcon Simulator

Grumman G-21 Goose

J-3 Cub

Mooney 21 Ranger

Piper PA-28-140 Cherokee

Piper PA-28-151 Warrior

Piper PA-28-181 Cherokee Archer

Piper PA-28R-200 Arrow

Piper PA-31-350 Navajo Chieftain

Piper PA-32-300 Cherokee Six

Piper PA-32R-301 Saratoga

In Memory of

H.R. (Dick) Lippincott 86

My beloved father not only gave his permission for me to pursue aviation but also was my primary facilitator. Dad supplied the aircraft, the runway, and the gas. It became a family affair. He made my early flight instruction possible and encouraged my pursuit of all things aviation, To this day, I feel his love any time that I am in the air or even thinking about taking to the skies. My motto for him will always be *nulli secundus,* which is Latin for "second to none." T. S. Elliott summed up my father's legacy, which lives on in my family, "A man is not dead until he is forgotten."

Carl I. Sisskind 84

I wish to acknowledge my very first aerial influence. Carl was a private pilot, TV personality, and a relative by marriage who gave me my first exposure to the world of flight. He ignited the aviation spark in me when he gave me my first plane ride at the tender age of five; I never saw him again after that trip. But those two hours spent together in 1955 left an indelible impression on me. Carl passed away in 2013 in San Diego, California.

Dale M. Walters 90

Dale was the Ryan Air no-frills station manager in Kotzebue, Alaska, who gave me my big break. Known as the "Arctic Grouch," he taught me how to survive those critical and stressful times during that first hard winter north of the Arctic Circle in 1989-90. As the chief pilot in Kotzebue, Dale drew on his half century of military and civilian aviation experience in his daily operations. I looked up to Dale and knew that he would test me in more ways than I could imagine. Dale passed away from complications of a hip fracture.

John R. Hitz 28

John succumbed to fatal injuries sustained in a motor vehicle accident on January 8, 1993. He joined Larry's Flying Service during the winter of 1992-3 and took up residence in a local log cabin with no running water. John had electricity but cut and burned firewood for heat. Not only was he likable, but also he was a fellow Nebraskan. Hitz was a young and carefree soul who loved life and had a passion for flying and adventure. I was excited to watch him grow and share in his Alaskan experience. He was doing what he loved when he was unfortunately killed.

Glossary

100LL - indicates aviation fuel, 100 octane and low lead.

A-6 Intruder - a carrier-based Navy plane designed as an all-weather medium attack jet aircraft.

Abeam - adjacent to or at right angles from a specified point.

ADF - stands for **A**utomatic **D**irection **F**inder used for non-precision navigation.

Air America - the CIA used a large civilian air force for operations during the Vietnam conflict.

Air Taxi Pilot - or FAR part 135 commercial flight rules.

AGL - **A**bove **G**round **L**evel. See also **MSL**.

ALCAN Highway - Alaska-Canadian Highway, 1,700 miles long built by the U.S. Army to connect the lower 48 with Alaska through Canada during World War II.

ANWR - **A**rctic **N**ational **W**ildlife **R**efuge, located in northeastern Alaska.

Arctic Circle - an imaginary line, 66° 30' north latitude denoting the northern border of the temperate zone.

ASRS - refers to the **A**viation **S**afety **R**eporting **S**ystem form to self-report a potential violation and receive forgiveness from the FAA. See also **NASA** form.

Astraphobic - an abnormal fear of lightning and thunder.

ATC - **A**ir **T**raffic **C**ontrol, sometimes called "Center." They are the guys watching radar screens and maintaining traffic separation in the clouds. The contiguous U.S. is divided into 21 areas of coverage like Minneapolis, Chicago, Atlanta, Los Angeles, and Albuquerque. ATC includes ground, tower, departure, approach, and center control.

ATIS - **A**ir **T**raffic **I**nformation **S**ervice, typically recorded every hour to update the pilot as to the current relevant conditions on the airfield like wind, visibility, active runway, etc.

ATP - for the highest pilot rating, the **A**irline **T**ransport **P**ilot, the minimum requirements are 1,500 hours pilot-in-command time, a twin-engine, instrument, and a commercial license.

Base Leg - part of the traffic pattern at 90 degrees to the final approach to the runway.

Breakup - this Alaskan term denotes the coming of spring as ice "breaks up" and is swept downstream and melting snow turns into mud.

Boneyard - adjacent to Davis-Monthan Air Force Base in Tucson, Arizona, the Boneyard is where the Air Force parks all of its old airplanes to be scrapped or mothballed for later use.

Bravo Airspace - Class B Airspace is the Terminal Control Area (TCA) in large metropolitan areas.

Caterpillar Pin - denotes someone who has made an emergency bailout of an aircraft.

CAVU - **C**lear **A**nd **V**isibility **U**nrestricted, good weather.

Centripetal force - any force responsible for maintaining an object on a curved path around a fixed center.

Centrifugal force - any force drawing a rotating body away from the center of rotation, caused by the inertia of the body, equal and opposite to the centripetal force.

CFIT - **C**ontrolled **F**light **I**nto **R**ising **T**errain. The second leading cause of air crash deaths or about 23 percent of all air related fatalities.

Chaff - metallic strips ejected from a military aircraft to confuse radar signals.

Checkride - flight, taken with an FAA-designated examiner for a license, rating, or currency.

Col - a saddle in a mountain ridge between two peaks.

Cold-shock - diving an airplane without power, therefore allowing the engine to cool too rapidly.

Contrail - a vapor track across the sky produced by heating humid air through an engine, thereby turning it into visible moisture.

Crabbing - in the air, pointing one way, but going another; moving sideways across the ground due to a strong crosswind.

CTAF - **C**ommon **T**raffic **A**rea **F**requency. May be the tower frequency when the tower is closed.

D-4 Caterpillar - a medium-size tractor or dozer with tracks and a blade in front.

Dead-reckoning - or pilotage, a method of navigation using a watch and compass (with an estimated ground speed).

Density Altitude - aircraft performance adjusted for standard day — temperature (59° Fahrenheit) and barometric pressure (29.92 in/ Hg), relative to sea level.

DEW Line - **D**istant **E**arly **W**arning **Line** radar erected during the cold war to detect incoming missiles from the USSR.

DG - directional gyro or non-magnetic compass.

DME - electronic **D**istance **M**easuring **E**quipment commonly used in aircraft for navigation.

Downwind Leg - part of the traffic pattern, going with the wind, which is the opposite direction of the Final Approach that is into the wind.

E6B Computer - nicknamed the "whiz wheel," it is like a circular slide rule, used in aviation training to solve navigation problems; it is one of the few analog computers still in use.

ELT - **E**mergency **L**ocator **T**ransponder, a radio device that is triggered at the time of a crash.

ETA - **E**stimated **T**ime of **A**rrival.

FAA - **F**ederal **A**viation **A**dministration, a government agency regulating flying.

FAR - **F**ederal **A**viation **R**egulations, the rules according to the FAA.

Feather - moving the propeller blades parallel to the airflow to reduce drag due to an engine failure. See also **Pitch.**

Final Leg - the terminal portion of the traffic pattern just before landing into the wind.

Flat Spin - a spin in an aircraft with the center of gravity in the extreme aft limits.

G-force - or G, the gravitational constant, one time the exertion of your body weight or gravity.

Gendarmes - the French term for a pinnacle or isolated rock tower frequently encountered along a ridge that tends to arrest a climbers progress.

Glory - the sunlight refracted around an aircraft shadow cast on a cloud with a distinctive rainbow ring or halo around it called a "glory."

GMO - **G**enetically **M**odified **O**rganism.

Glideslope - an electronic beam generated from near the end of the runway, detectable on instruments in the cockpit, used to navigate during the approach to landing.

Glissade - to ski downhill on rock or snow standing on your feet or sitting on your buttocks.

GPS - **G**lobal **P**ositioning **S**ystem, a space-based navigation system; commissioned in 1973 it used Cesium-133 as an atomic clock to calculate time and location on Earth. The system was not fully operational until 1995.

Ground Effect - the aircraft wing can "push" against the runway for additional lift up to an altitude equal to the length of the wing. Waterfowl routinely do this on the water.

Hemispheric Rules - VFR traffic eastbound will fly at odd numbered altitudes plus 500 feet, and westbound planes will fly at even numbered altitudes plus 500 feet above 3,000 feet. All IFR traffic is assigned to the cardinal altitudes.

IFR - **I**nstrument **F**light **R**ules. Regulations for flying in the clouds and above 18,000 feet.

ILS - precision **I**nstrument **L**anding **S**ystem; provides vertical and lateral guidance down to 200 feet off the runway.

IMC - **I**nstrument **M**eteorologic **C**onditions, or in the clouds and loss of the horizon.

IOE - **I**nitial **O**perating **E**xperience, to learn the procedures and routes for an air carrier.

Jug - an engine cylinder including the head, valves, and piston.

Lend-Lease Program - the Arctic route through Fairbanks, Alaska, and Canada were the shortest and most dangerous for war aid to the USSR. The Arctic route supplied 23 percent of the total aid to the USSR. Losses totaled an astounding 7 percent of the goods and aircraft transported.

Magnetic Declination - is the difference between true north and magnetic north and may be positive or negative. Currently, it is moving northwest about 35 miles per year.

Marston Matting - World War II Air Corps name was PSP for perforated steel planking, used for constructing portable runways. The name came from Marston, North Carolina, adjacent to the Camp Mackall Airfield, where it was first used.

MEA - Minimum Enroute Altitude, provides for terrain separation, communication, and navigation.

Metal Fatigue - the weakening of a material caused by repeated loads.

Microburst - a strong downward vertical blast of air from a thunderstorm that spreads out in 360 degrees once it hits the ground. See also **Williwaw**.

Monument Valley - a portion of the Navajo nation with iconic sandstone monoliths and formations.

Moulins - ice caves in glaciers created by meltwater; they are both vertical and horizontal.

MSL - Mean Sea Level, distance above the surface of the ocean. See also **AGL**.

NASA - The National Aeronautics and Space Administration, the Aviation Safety Reporting System form to self-report a potential violation and receive forgiveness from the FAA. See also **ASRS**.

NEO - Near-Earth Objects or asteroids.

North Slope - the flat coastal plain north of the Brooks Range to the Beaufort Sea.

NTSB - National Transportation Safety Board investigates aviation accidents.

OAT - the aeronautical term for Outside Air Temperature.

Outside - term Alaskans use when they refer to the "Lower 48."

Ozone - a pungent, distinctly caustic odor generated by atmospheric electrical discharges, it can be smelled in the air following a lightning discharge. The upper layer of the ozone protects the Earth from 99 percent of UV radiation. The same high-energy ultraviolet light from the Sun interacts with stratospheric oxygen generating the very same ozone.

Pack Ice - polar sea ice that has been pushed together by wind and currents.

Phlegmon - an area of infected tissue that has not formed an abscess requiring surgical drainage.

Pilot-In-Command (PIC) - the pilot with the final say and ultimate responsibility for the flight.

Pitch - a section of a climb, usually one rope length. On a propeller, it is the angle of the blade's bite taken in the air. Fine pitch on takeoff, course for cruise flight, and zero pitch to feather. See also **Feather.**

Rime ice - slow growing ice that is smooth, homogeneous, opaque, and milky white.

Rotors - strong downdrafts on the lee side of a ridge or mountain, or blades on a helicopter.

Round-Robin - the entire trip, to the destination and back to the starting point.

Runway - landing surface that is paved, gravel, dirt, water, snow, or grass field.

RW - **R**elative **W**ork, in freefall it refers to maneuvers with one or more other skydivers.

Service Ceiling - the maximum usable altitude for a particular aircraft.

Single Pilot IFR - high workload flight in the clouds with only one pilot at the controls.

Skidder - a type of heavy track-type vehicle used in a logging operation for pulling cut trees out of a forest in a process called "skidding," in which the logs are towed from the cutting site for processing.

Sleds - a colloquialism for Ryan Air red Cessna 207 aircraft.

SNL - **S**aturday **N**ight **L**ive, TV comedy program.

Snowmachine - the Alaskan term for Snowmobile.

Sputnik - Russia placed the first satellite in orbit. It traveled at 18,000 mph for a total of three months before it fell back to earth.

Squawk - descrete transponder code used for aircraft radar identification.

Sublimate - when ice turns to vapor, skipping the liquid or water phase. Like ice cubes in your freezer that evaporate or shrink over time.

Supercharger - a mechanically driven compressor used to inject a greater volume of oxygen into the engine. See also **Turbocharger**.

Taiga - subarctic zone of evergreen coniferous forests situated south of the tundra region in the Northern Hemisphere.

TCA - **T**erminal **C**ontrol **A**rea. Now called Class B airspace around large busy cities.

Tesseract - the tesseract is the four-dimensional analog of the cube; the tesseract is to the cube as the cube is to the square. A line has one dimension, a square has two, a cube has three, and a tesseract has four dimensions.

Three Dog Night - a reference to using a dog's body heat to help survive a cold evening - you need more animals on the coldest nights.

Tok - a town in northeastern Alaska on the ALCAN Highway. Some say that it was the "T" intersection on an early map, and when approved, an OK was added by some official and the name stuck.

Trench or The Canadian Trench - a trans-Canadian route along a valley running north/south between Watson Lake and Mackenzie. The southern half is Lake Williston.

Trim tab - small adjustable surfaces connected to the trailing edge of a larger control surface to counteract aerodynamic forces without the need for the pilot to continually apply pressure to the control yoke.

TSO - **T**echnical **S**tandard **O**rder - a minimum performance standard for specified materials, parts, and appliances used on civil aircraft.

Turbocharger - an exhaust driven, mechanical fan used to inject compressed air into the engine. See also **Supercharger**.

Valdez Ice Festival - an informal ice climbing tournament hosted by Andy Embic MD. Most of the participants stayed at his house in Valdez for the entire event.

VFR - **V**isual **F**light **R**ules - Federal laws for flight with visual reference outside of the aircraft.

VOR - **V**ery High-Frequency **O**mnidirectional **R**adio beacon, used for line-of-sight aviation navigation.

Williwaw - a sudden strong blast of wind (cold, dense air from snow or ice fields) descending from a mountain slope to the sea. See also **Microburst.**

Wright Brothers Master Pilot Award - FAA award for 50 years of continuous safe aviation.

Printed in the United States
By Bookmasters